FEASTING on FOOD STORAGE

Delicious *and* Healthy Recipes *for* Everyday Cooking

Jane P. Merrill
Karen M. Sunderland

FRONT TABLE BOOKS

An Imprint of Cedar Fort, Inc.
Springville, Utah

ISBN 13: 978-1-4621-1289-0

Published by Front Table Books, an imprint of Cedar Fort, Inc.
2373 W. 700 S., Springville, UT 84663
Distributed by Cedar Fort, Inc., www.cedarfort.com

Library of Congress Cataloging-in-Publication Data on file

Cover and page design by Erica Dixon
Cover design © 2013 by Lyle Mortimer

Printed in the United States of America

10 9 8 7 6 5 4 3 2 1

Contents

ACKNOWLEDGMENTS

We express love and gratitude to Jay W. Merrill, dear husband and father and a constant source of strength and encouragement, whose support has never wavered through all the many challenges we have surmounted! We also express deep appreciation to all those who have given so willingly of their time and talent in the preparation of this book.

INTRODUCTION

Feasting on Food Storage is a unique book, featuring hundreds of appetizing, easy-to-use recipes that incorporate basic storage foods in such a way that your family will enjoy eating them. These family-tested recipes will also help transition you into using items from your longer-term food storage. Eating storage foods more frequently helps rotate your food supply, saves money, and supports health, as well as keeps you prepared for any emergency.

Included are chapters with easy and delicious recipes, chapters like "Gluten-Free is Here to Stay" and "Baby Food Made Easy." The concluding chapters—"Emergency Cooking Solutions," "The Sick Bay," and "Prepare for the Unexpected"—contain a concise compilation of pertinent, hard-to-find emergency preparedness solutions. They also include practical guidelines and suggestions for dealing with emergencies of all kinds to help you survive the unexpected situation that may arise.

Feasting on Food Storage is the result of a combined mother-daughter team effort. Jane P. Merrill and Karen M. Sunderland, authors of the best-selling lifestyle cookbook *Set for Life*, bring you another practical, must-have book that will enrich your life.

CHAPTER 1

Now Is the Time to Prepare!

When an Emergency Arises, the Time For Preparation Is Past

In ancient times, a universal calamity caused the destruction of all mankind except one man and his family of eight. They had tried for years to get their friends, neighbors, and everyone else to heed God's warnings, but to no avail. Noah and his family boarded the ark with their food and supplies, and they were spared. In our day, no one knows exactly what disasters we may have to face, but if we are wise, we will follow counsel and prepare now with the food and supplies we would need to survive any calamity that may arise.

Being prepared for the unexpected doesn't mean preparing for just one major disaster. It means being prepared for any challenge life may offer. Many of these are taking place today, such as major inflation, wildfires, floods, power outages, erratic weather patterns, food shortages, a sagging economy, political upheaval, injury, unemployment, and so on.

In today's uncertain world, being prepared for an unexpected emergency is just good common sense. For many years, we have been advised to supply ourselves with extra food, clothing, and, if possible, fuel. Those who have followed these guidelines have been able to weather difficult circumstances and have peace of mind knowing they can take care of their own needs in case of misfortune or other unforeseen events. Prepare for the unexpected, and *now* is the time to do it!

» What Is Food Storage?

"Food storage is any food stored to be eaten at a later time—4 hours, 4 days, or 4 years. Food storage is any food in the refrigerator, in the freezer, on the shelf, in the garden, on the tree, livestock, etc." (Utah State University Cooperative Extension, *"Use It or Lose It!"*, 3-1). When acquiring food storage, be sure to choose foods that your family can and will eat. Be aware that eating right decreases fatigue, increases energy and endurance, prevents dehydration, maintains mental alertness, reduces diarrhea and constipation, reduces risk of injury, and maintains morale and strength. In extreme conditions, what and how much you eat and drink can mean the difference between life and death, so store wisely! Store what you eat and eat what you store. Contrary to what most of us would like to believe, food does not keep forever, nor does it improve with age. Continually use and replace the foods in your storage to assure freshness, while maintaining an adequate supply. Rotating food is often the most difficult part of home storage, but it is important. Freeze-dried and dehydrated foods are a highly recommended addition to your basic long-term food storage. Most of them are packaged to keep twenty to thirty years or more, but you can start using them now, such as adding dried fruit to oatmeal, muffins, pancakes, granola, and so on. Storing and using a wide variety of freeze-dried and dehydrated vegetables and meats will help meet the nutritional needs of your family. They make flavorful additions to soups and stews, and they add fiber, vitamins, and minerals. Find your family favorites, add them to your food storage, and start using them. Store plenty of additional water when including freeze-dried and dehydrated foods as part of your storage. Space to store food can be a problem, so be creative. Add extra shelves in the tops of closets and use space under beds, behind sofas, in the basement, and in any other available areas. Cool, dark, and dry storage conditions are best to preserve nutrition and quality. Where there's a will, there's a way!

» Getting Started Is as Simple as 1, 2, 3 . . .

FIRST: Inventory all the food you have on hand. Next, see what meals can be prepared using those foods. Determine how long you could survive on the foods you currently have. Evaluate where you are and where you want and need to be. Categorize your inventory list and keep it updated.

SECOND: Gather a supply of storable food that you typically eat, foods that are part of your normal daily diet. Focus on canned and commercially packaged foods that have a stable shelf life. Start with acquiring a one-week supply, followed by two, three, and then four weeks. Continue following this plan. Buy what staples you usually eat, but begin purchasing two or more at a time. This will increase your supply quite rapidly, and it will soon be sufficient for three months. Include basics such as flour, sugar, oil, yeast, baking powder, and baking soda, plus condiments and seasonings, so you can make your own baked goods if necessary. Keeping your pantry well stocked and organized saves both time and money. You will love the convenience of having the right foods on hand when you need them to prepare a meal.

THIRD: Be a time and money super saver. Here's how:

1. Plan ahead. Consider that the average family eats only eight to ten different dinner menus repeatedly. So make a list of eight or more basic main meal menus you enjoy and can easily prepare. Include favorite soups, stews, and casseroles that are simple, nutritious, and food storage friendly. A sample plan to help you get started is included herein.

2. Shop the sales. Use some of these menus each week, based on foods you have on hand and foods on sale at your favorite stores. By planning menus around weekly sales ads, you can often save 30 percent or more on an average grocery bill and really stretch your food dollars. Design these meals to fit your own family. Fix at least one meal each week using some of your longer-term storage foods so you all get used to eating them.

3. Use your menus as a guide. Check your refrigerator, freezer, and pantry to see which items you already have on hand. Make a list of any additional items you will need. You can make a master grocery list following the configuration of your favorite grocery store and keep copies ready to use. Then simply check each item you want and write in the amount needed. Habits rule our lives, so be consistent in planning and in following through with your plan.

4. Shop once a week and stick to your list. You can write your list on an envelope where coupons can be stashed for easy availability. When you use a can or package of some food item, put it on your grocery list and replace it. As you shop, buy at least two of the basic items needed instead of just one. In this way you will soon build up an adequate supply of foods you regularly use. When possible, stock up on quality nonperishable sale items that you plan to use in the next few months. Never compromise quality for price. Avoid dented cans and foods that are questionable in any way. However, use common sense as you rotate your foods inasmuch as some foods are safe to use long after the suggested use-by date.

5. Save time and money. Cook once and eat twice or more by doubling or tripling at least one recipe each week. Enjoy one for dinner and freeze a meal or two for later, with little or no extra effort. This keeps your freezer stocked with ready-to-eat meals for busy days. One-dish meals can also save money and time. Making your own breads and pastries saves big money. This is much easier to do if you have the right kitchen equipment, such as a Bosch mixer, a good blender, and an electric grain mill (adjustable is best). And the new safe pressure cookers are great time-saving appliances.

6. Don't panic or go into debt to get prepared! Most of us can't get everything we will need at one time, but we can begin, and *now* is the time. Simply start with getting a three-month food supply. You will save big if you plan ahead, make a list, and shop wisely. Always keep in mind that good nutrition is of the utmost importance during times of stress to increase energy and help avoid illness.

» Food Storage Meals

- -

12 Family Food Storage Meals • 3-Month Supply • 1 Meal 8 times

1. Spaghetti and Green Beans

One Meal	Eight Meals
1 (16-oz.) box spaghetti noodles	8 boxes spaghetti noodles
1 (24-oz.) can spaghetti sauce	8 cans spaghetti sauce
1 (14-oz.) can green beans	8 cans green beans

2. Chicken Broccoli Casserole

One Meal	Eight Meals
1 (6-oz.) packet stuffing mix	8 packets stuffing mix
1 (10-oz.) can cream of chicken soup	8 cans soup
1 chicken bouillon cube	8 bouillon cubes
1 (16-oz.) bag frozen broccoli	8 bags broccoli
1 (12-oz.) can chicken	8 cans chicken

3. Chicken Noodle Soup

One Meal	Eight Meals
3 (16-oz.) cans broth or 3 Tbsp. chicken bouillon	24 cans broth or 1½ cups bouillon
1 (10-oz.) can chicken	8 cans chicken
1 (14-oz.) can carrots	8 cans carrots
2 Tbsp. dry minced onion	1 cup dry minced onion
¼ cup celery or dehydrated celery	2–3 cups celery
1 envelope dry chicken noodle soup	8 envelopes dry chicken noodle soup

4. Taco Sundae Casserole

One Meal	Eight Meals
2 cups rice	8 (16-oz.) pkgs. rice
2 (14-oz.) cans chili with beans	16 cans chili with beans
1 (14-oz.) can pinto beans	8 cans pinto beans
1 (14-oz.) can corn	8 cans corn

5. Cabin Stew

One Meal	Eight Meals
1 (24-oz.) can stew	8 cans stew
1 (14-oz.) can chili with beans	8 cans chili with beans
1 (10-oz.) can vegetable beef soup	8 cans vegetable beef soup

6. Quick Enchilada Casserole

One Meal	Eight Meals
1 (10-oz.) can cream of chicken soup	8 cans cream of chicken soup
2 Tbsp. dry chopped onion	1 cup dry chopped onion
1 (4-oz.) can diced green chilies	8 cans diced green chilies
1–2 cups diced chicken, with liquid, optional	8 cans chicken, optional
12 corn tortillas, torn into large pieces	8 pkgs. of 12 tortillas
½ cup shredded cheese	4 cups shredded cheese

7. Hawaiian Haystacks

One Meal	Eight Meals
2 cups rice	8 (16-oz.) pkgs. rice
1 (10-oz.) can cream of chicken soup	8 cans cream of chicken soup
1 (12-oz.) can chicken	8 cans chicken
1 (20-oz.) can crushed pineapple	8 cans crushed pineapple
1 pkg. Chinese noodles	8 pkgs. Chinese noodles

8. Lentil Soup

One Meal	Eight Meals
1 (16-oz.) pkg. lentils	8 (16-oz.) pkgs. lentils
2 Tbsp. dry chopped onion	1 cup dry chopped onion
2 chicken or beef bouillon cubes	16 chicken or beef bouillon cubes
1 (24-oz.) spaghetti sauce	8 (24-oz.) cans spaghetti sauce

9. Fiesta Bake

One Meal	Eight Meals
1 Tbsp. minced garlic	½ cup minced garlic
2 Tbsp. dry chopped onion	1 cup dry chopped onion
1 (10-oz.) can enchilada sauce	8 cans enchilada sauce
1 (8-oz.) can tomato sauce	8 cans tomato sauce
2 (14-oz.) cans chili with beans	16 cans chili with beans
1 (14-oz.) can corn	8 cans corn
10 corn tortillas	8 pkgs. of 10 corn tortillas

10. Tuna or Chicken Noodle Casserole

One Meal	Eight Meals
2 (5-oz.) cans tuna or chicken	16 cans tuna or chicken
1 (10-oz.) can cream of chicken soup	8 cans cream of chicken soup
2 Tbsp. dry chopped onion	1 cup dry chopped onion
1 cup frozen broccoli or peas	8 cups frozen broccoli or peas
3 cups dry crinkle noodles	24 cups (5 lbs.) dry noodles

11. Split Pea Soup

One Meal	Eight Meals
1 (16-oz.) pkg. split peas	8 (16-oz.) pkgs. split peas
2 Tbsp. dry chopped onion	1 cup dry chopped onion
1 (14-oz) can potatoes	8 cans potatoes
1 (14-oz.) can carrots	8 cans carrots
3 stalks celery or ¼ cup dehydrated celery	24 stalks celery or 2 cups dehydrated
1 (5-oz.) can ham	8 cans ham

12. Nine-Bean Soup

One Meal	Eight Meals
1 (16-oz.) pkg. nine-bean soup mix	8 pkgs. nine-bean soup mix
1 (5-oz.) can ham	8 cans ham
2 Tbsp. dry chopped onion	1 cup dry chopped onion
1 Tbsp. minced garlic	½ cup minced garlic
1 (4-oz.) can diced green chilies	8 cans diced green chilies
1 (14-oz.) can diced tomatoes	8 cans tomatoes
3 Tbsp. lemon juice	1½ cups lemon juice

» Store Water

Drinking water is absolutely vital for survival! Store drinking water for circumstances in which your water supply may be polluted or disrupted. Water from a chlorinated municipal water supply does not need further treatment when stored in clean, food-grade containers.

Store water in sturdy, leak-proof, breakage-resistant food-grade containers. Clean plastic juice bottles and soda bottles or smaller containers made of PET plastic work well. Plastic milk or bleach containers are not recommended. Keep water containers away from heat and direct sunlight. Small, efficient water purification filters are available at many recreation and outdoor stores. Water purification tablets are also available. These come with an expiration date, which should be noted since they can become ineffective with time.

To store water from a non-chlorinated source: Fill a clean two-liter bottle to the top with regular tap water. If the water you are using comes from a well or water source that is not treated with chlorine, add two drops of fresh non-scented liquid household chlorine bleach to the water. Tightly close the container using the original cap. Be careful not to contaminate the cap by touching the inside of it with your finger. Place a date on the outside of the container so that you know when you filled it. Store water in a cool, dark place. Replace the water every six months if not using commercially bottled water.

» Longer-Term Food Supply

For longer-term needs, gradually build up a supply of staple foods that will last a long time, such as whole grains, white rice, legumes, sugar, and salt. These items can last thirty years or more when properly packaged—such as in #10 tin cans with an oxygen absorber packet or in airtight food-grade buckets—and stored in a cool, dry place. Whole grains and beans are nutritious, low-stress, high-energy foods that are high in fiber and low in fat. They help strengthen the body and keep it healthy. A varied diet of beans, lentils, grains, and vegetables contains all of the essential amino acids. People once thought that various plant foods had to be eaten together to get their full protein value, but current research suggests this is not the case. As long as you are eating a variety of plant foods in sufficient quantity to maintain your weight, your body gets plenty of protein.

These essential foods sustain life over a long period of time, store well, take limited storage space, and are relatively inexpensive. Most vegetables can be grown in a small space, but the staples listed require large amounts of land, a longer growing season, and heavy equipment to harvest. In a disaster they are often the most difficult to obtain, so keep a good supply on hand.

» Basic Long-Term Food Storage For 1 Adult

Food Supply	Per Day	Per Year
Wheat/grains	2¼ cups	400 lbs.
Wheat, oats, rice, corn, popcorn, barley, flour, spaghetti, macaroni, etc.		
Vegetable oils/fats	3 Tbsp.	4 gallons
Oil, shortening, peanut butter, mayonnaise, salad dressings, etc.		
Beans/legumes	⅓ cup	60 lbs.
Dry beans, split peas, lentils, dry soup mix, etc.		
Powdered milk	1½ tablespoons	16 lbs
Nonfat dry milk, evaporated milk (6 cans = 1 lb.), etc.		
Sugars or honey	⅓ cup	60 lbs.
White sugar, brown sugar, powdered sugar, honey, maple syrup, molasses, jam, jelly, corn syrup, powdered fruit drink, flavored gelatin, etc.		
Salt	3 tsp.	10 lbs.
Store in original containers.		
Water	1 gallon minimum	365 gallons
Store a minimum 2-week supply of water (Franz, Maintaining Nutritional Adequacy, 84).		

- Baking necessities: baking powder, baking soda, dry yeast, cornstarch
- Garden seeds, non-hybrid recommended
- Sprouting seeds, untreated
- Heavy-duty nonelectric can openers
- Nonstick cooking sprays
- Cider and white vinegar

- Medications as needed

- Multivitamins, vitamin C, etc.

- Baby foods and formula, if needed

- Fruits

- Vegetables

- Meats; frozen, canned, and dried

- Soups; frozen, canned, and dried

- Condiments and seasonings (choose family favorites), like basil, beef and chicken bouillon, catsup, cayenne pepper, chili powder, cinnamon, cloves, cocoa, cream of tartar, cumin, dillseed, dill weed, garlic (minced, powder, and salt), ginger, Italian seasoning, maple flavoring, marjoram, mustard (regular and dry), nutmeg, dry onion, onion salt, oregano, paprika, parsley, pepper, poultry seasoning, ranch dressing mix, sage, salsa, seasoned salt, soy sauce, taco seasoning, thyme, vanilla, Worcestershire sauce, etc.

» KEEP YOUR PANTRY & REFRIGERATOR WELL STOCKED

Perishables: Use It or Lose It

butter	frozen fruit	mayonnaise
cheese	frozen vegetables	milk
eggs	frozen meats	salad dressing
flaxseed and meal	margarine	fresh vegetables
fresh fruit		

Baking Basics

baking powder	coconut	raisins and Craisins
baking soda	cornstarch	whole wheat flour
dry yeast	corn syrup	white flour
brown sugar	dry milk	cornmeal
white sugar	evaporated milk	salt
powdered sugar	honey	shortening
cake mixes	molasses	vegetable oil
canned frosting	marshmallows	nonstick cooking spray
chocolate chips	oats; quick, regular	
nuts		
cocoa		

Spice It Up

Condiments and spices are essential for tasty eating

basil	ginger	poultry seasoning
beef bouillon	Italian seasoning	pumpkin pie spice
chicken bouillon	maple flavoring	ranch dressing mix
catsup	marjoram	sage
cayenne	mustard	salt
chili powder	nutmeg	seasoned salt
cinnamon	dry chopped onion	salsa
cloves	onion salt	soy sauce
cream of tartar	and powder	taco seasoning
cumin	oregano	thyme
dill weed	paprika	vanilla
garlic powder	parsley	worcestershire
and salt	pepper	sauce

On the Shelf

apple cider vinegar, white vinegar, etc.	pasta: elbow, penne, lasagna, spaghetti, etc.	canned soups and stews
flavored gelatin		canned beans: black, garbanzo, kidney, pinto, pork 'n beans, refried, white
instant puddings	peanut butter	
jams, jellies, etc.	garlic	

On the Shelf (continued):

fruits of choice: applesauce, apricots, peaches, pears, pineapples, etc.	onions, tomatoes (crushed, diced, stewed, etc.), etc.	ham
	salsa	salmon
		tuna
vegetables of choice: corn, green beans, green chilies, mushrooms, pumpkins,	tomato sauce and tomato paste	baby foods, as needed
	alfredo sauce	multivitamins etc.
	spaghetti sauce	medications, as needed
	chicken	salt

Dry Grains, Legumes, etc.

wheat	barley	black beans
brown rice	lentils	pinto beans
white rice	split peas	white beans
popcorn		

» Wheat

The wheat kernel or wheat berry is the seed of the wheat plant and is power-packed with the food nutrients needed and used by man for thousands of years. Wheat is rich in protein, vitamins B and E, and many minerals. When sprouted it also supplies vitamins A and C, so it's a balanced storehouse of nutrients that help build a strong, healthy body. In addition, whole wheat is high in fiber, which is vital to good health. Wheat is called the universal grain. It serves as the staple food for over half the world's population and is the primary grain used in United States grain products (National Association of Wheat Growers, "Fast Facts").

Not all wheat is created equal, so be selective when choosing wheat for storage. Clean, dry, hard white or hard red wheat with a protein content of 14 percent or higher is best. The moisture content should be 10 percent or less. If properly stored in moisture-proof containers in a cool dry place, this type of wheat should store indefinitely and remain high in nutrients.

Hard wheat is superior for making high-quality yeast breads. It can also be used in making quick breads, cookies, cakes, bulgur, and so on. Wheat is a versatile grain and can be cooked, sprouted, and used to grow wheat grass. Directions for all these uses of wheat are included herein.

When a food product contains whole grains such as whole wheat, oats, barley, or rye, all of the nutrients can be utilized in the balance nature intended. Whole grains often reduce the risk of many major diseases, such as cardiovascular disease, and many chronic diseases such as diabetes and cancer, and they provide energy for daily activities and long-term wellness.

For people who are wheat intolerant, many alternatives are available. When wheat is used in our recipes, you can substitute other grains. For yeasted breads, if you don't have celiac disease (gluten intolerant), you can use spelt flour as a wheat alternative. See chapter 3 for gluten-free baking and cooking ideas. Chefbrad.com has further information on gluten intolerance. With a little work and creativity, you can easily adapt recipes in this book to fit your needs. There is wisdom in storing an assortment of grains that offer a variety of nutrients and flavor to your diet.

» Bulgur

Bulgur is a precooked, dried cracked wheat. It is easy to make and use.

To Make Bulgur

Cook whole wheat until tender using any of the methods given herein. Spread the cooked wheat in a thin layer on baking sheets and dry thoroughly in a 200-degree oven or hot sun until very dry. This will take several hours. A dehydrator may also be used. When dry, crack bulgur slightly using a blender or hand grinder, or it can be left whole. Store bulgur in covered jars. Bulgur stores well on the shelf and is ready to rehydrate and eat in minutes.

To Use Bulgur

1 part bulgur   2 parts water

Bring water and bulgur to a boil, cover, and simmer for 10–15 minutes, or until tender. Bulgur approximately doubles in volume when cooked and is ready to use immediately. When tightly covered, it will keep in the refrigerator for up to two weeks.

Bulgur is probably the easiest whole wheat food to prepare and certainly ranks as one of the most versatile foods in use. None of the measurements are critical, and there's no fussing with stirring, continual watching, and so on.

Bulgur gives an interesting flavor and texture to foods in which it is used. Use bulgur as a hot cereal. Add to most any soup, stew, or salad. Try adding a little to chicken or tuna sandwich fillings. Bulgur is an excellent meat extender in meat loaf, casseroles, pilaf, and other main dishes. It can substitute for mashed potatoes, or it can be baked to make a nutritious crunchy snack. It can also be added to muffins, salads, or desserts. Bulgur is versatile *and* nutritious.

» Wheat and Flour Equivalents

One #10 can of wheat equals approximately:

- 6 lbs. or 14 cups of wheat
- 21 cups of flour
- 7 large loaves of raised bread
- 10–12 loaves of quick bread
- 10 batches of pancakes
- 10 batches of biscuits
- 10 batches of chocolate chip or other cookies

Five pounds of flour equals approximately:

- 18 cups of flour
- 6 large loaves of raised bread
- 8–9 loaves of quick bread
- 8–9 batches of pancakes
- 8–9 batches of biscuits
- 7–8 batches of chocolate chip or other cookies

Figure out about how many loaves of yeast or quick bread, pancakes, biscuits, or cookies you make in a week. Multiply that amount times four to see how much flour you use in a month. Multiply that number by three months and you will know about how much flour you will need in your three-month supply. During hard times you will be baking more frequently, so store generously!

White flour stores approximately one year in an airtight container before going stale.

White flour stored in a sealed #10 can with an oxygen absorber packet will store for about ten years in a dry place at or below 75 degrees.

Wheat stores thirty-plus years in a closed container. Four hundred pounds of wheat equals about sixty-seven #10 cans.

» Equivalent Measurements

Amount	Equal to	Equal to
A pinch	⅛ teaspoon or less	
3 teaspoons	1 tablespoon	½ ounce
2 tablespoons	⅛ cup	1 ounce
4 tablespoons	¼ cup	2 ounces
5⅓ tablespoons	⅓ cup	
8 tablespoons	½ cup	4 ounces
12 tablespoons	¾ cup	6 ounces
16 tablespoons	1 cup	8 ounces
24 tablespoons	1 ½ cups	12 ounces
2 cups	1 pint	16 ounces
4 cups	1 quart	32 ounces
2 pints	1 quart	32 ounces
4 quarts	1 gallon	128 ounces

» Oven Temperatures

Slow moderate...**325°F**

Moderate...**350°F**

Hot..**425°F**

Very hot...**450 to 475°F**

» Approximate Equivalent Ingredient Measurements

Ingredient	Amount	Equal to
Apple	1 medium	1 cup, sliced or diced
Bread	3–4 slices	1 cup crumbs
Butter	1 stick	½ cup
Cheese	¼ pound	1 cup, shredded
Dates	1 cup	2½ cups, chopped
Dry beans	½ cup	2½ cups, cooked
Eggs	5 medium	1 cup
Graham crackers	14 squares	1 cup fine crumbs
Lemon	1 medium	3–4 tablespoons juice
Macaroni, spaghetti	1 cup uncooked	2 cups, cooked
Noodles	1 cup uncooked	1 cup cooked
Nuts, chopped	4–5 ounces	1 cup
Onion	1 medium	½ cup
Orange	1 medium	⅓ to ½ cup juice
Rice	1 cup, uncooked	3½ cups, cooked
Rice, instant	1 cup	2 cups, cooked
Soda crackers	18–20	1 cup medium crumbs

CHAPTER 2

The Bakery

» QUICK BREADS

Homemade quick breads give a wonderful lift to even the simplest meal. These breads are popular because they're quick and easy to prepare. Hot breads make any meal special.

Two cups of whole wheat kernels makes about 3 cups of ground flour. Cup for cup, whole wheat flour may be substituted for white flour. All whole wheat or all white flour may be used in any of these recipes. Gluten-free flour can be used in lieu of regular flour in these recipes.

Favorite Muffins

Yield: 14 to 16 muffins

Try these tender, light muffins. You'll enjoy the flavorful variations too.

2 cups flour, whole wheat or white

½ cup sugar or honey

1 Tbsp. baking powder

½ tsp. salt

1 cup milk, or 1 scant cup water and ¼ cup dry milk

1 egg, slightly beaten

⅓ cup oil

Preheat oven to 400°F. Mix flour, sugar, baking powder, and salt. If using dry milk, mix it with dry ingredients. Whisk in milk or water along with the egg and oil. Mix only until flour is moistened. Fill greased muffin pans almost full and bake for 12–15 minutes.

Blueberry Muffins: Decrease milk or water by ¼ cup. Toss 1 cup fresh or frozen blueberries with 3 tablespoons sugar. Fold into batter and bake.

Raisin, Nut, or Date Muffins: Add ½ cup raisins, chopped nuts, or chopped dates. Stir quickly into batter and bake.

Apple-Raisin Muffins: Fold in 1 cup shredded or chopped apples and ½ cup raisins.

Oat Bran Muffins

Yield: 18 muffins

Mix and bake these moist, delicious muffins in minutes. High in soluble and insoluble fiber, they help lower cholesterol and are a pleasant way to "stay regular."

½ cup very hot water

1 cup 100% bran cereal or wheat or oat bran

½ cup rolled oats

½ cup raisins, chopped

1 cup milk, or 1 cup water and ¼ cup dry milk

1 Tbsp. vinegar

1 egg, slightly beaten

¼ cup oil or applesauce

1 cup whole wheat flour

⅓ cup white flour

⅓ cup sugar

1 tsp. baking soda

1 tsp. salt

Preheat oven to 400°F. Stir hot water into bran and rolled oats. Chop raisins in blender with milk or water and add to bran mix. Let mixture stand a few minutes to soften ingredients. Stir in vinegar, egg, and oil or applesauce. Mix flours, sugar, baking soda, and salt. If using dry milk, mix into dry ingredients. Add dry mixture to bran mixture and stir only until ingredients are moistened. Fill greased muffin pans almost full and bake for 14–16 minutes.

Brown Sugar Muffins

Yield: 12 to 14 muffins

½ cup oil

1 cup brown sugar

1 egg, slightly beaten

1 cup milk, or 1 cup water and ¼ cup dry milk

1 tsp. vanilla

1 cup whole wheat flour

1 cup white flour

1 tsp. baking soda

½ tsp. salt

½ cup nuts or raisins, optional

Preheat oven to 375°F. Mix brown sugar, egg, milk or water, and vanilla. Add flours, baking soda, and salt. If using dry milk, mix it into dry ingredients. Mix just until ingredients are combined but not smooth. Fold in nuts or raisins if desired. Fill greased muffin tins almost full. Sprinkle with more brown sugar if desired. Bake for 15–18 minutes.

Gingerbread Muffins

Yield: 15 to 18 muffins

Fragrant and spicy!

½ cup sugar

1 egg, well beaten

⅓ cup oil or shortening

½ cup molasses

2½ cups flour

1½ tsp. baking soda

½ tsp. salt

1 tsp. cinnamon

1 tsp. ginger

½ tsp. cloves

1 cup hot water

Preheat oven to 350°F. Beat sugar, egg, oil or shortening, and molasses until light and fluffy. Mix flour, baking soda, salt, cinnamon, ginger, and cloves. Add hot water alternately with dry ingredients. Mix just until smooth. Fill greased muffin pans almost full and bake. Bake for 12–15 minutes.

Gingerbread

Yield: 18 pieces

Preheat oven to 350°F. Follow Gingerbread Muffins recipe above but increase sugar to 1 cup. Pour into a greased 9×13 baking dish. Bake until toothpick inserted in center comes out clean, 25–30 minutes.

Biscuits Supreme

Yield: 16 biscuits

Light and fluffy biscuits make any meal special.

2 cups white flour, or 1 cup white flour and 1 cup whole wheat flour

1 Tbsp. baking powder

½ tsp. salt

¾ cup milk, or ¾ cup water and ¼ cup dry milk

¼ cup oil

Preheat oven to 425°F. Mix flour, baking powder, and salt. If using dry milk, mix into dry ingredients. Add milk or water and oil. Stir with a fork just until dough follows fork around bowl. Knead dough lightly on floured surface for about 30 seconds; too much handling makes biscuits tough. Roll or pat dough ½ inch thick. Cut into squares with pizza cutter. Bake on ungreased baking sheet for 10–12 minutes.

Stir 'n' Drop Biscuits

Yield: 16 to 18 biscuits

These also make a good topping for meat pie.

2 cups flour

1 Tbsp. sugar

1 Tbsp. baking powder

½ tsp. salt

1 cup milk, or 1 cup water and ¼ cup dry milk

1 egg, slightly beaten

¼ cup oil

Preheat oven to 425°F. Mix flour, sugar, baking powder, and salt. If using dry milk, mix into dry ingredients. Add milk or water, egg, and oil. Stir with a fork only until ingredients are combined. Fill greased muffins pans almost full or drop dough 1 inch apart on an ungreased baking sheet and bake for 12–14 minutes.

Baking Mix (like Bisquick)

Yield: 10 cups mix

This mix is quick and convenient.

9 cups flour
1 cup dry milk
⅓ cup baking powder

4 tsp. salt
1½ cups shortening

Mix flour, dry milk, baking powder, and salt. Cut shortening into dry ingredients. Store in airtight container in cool place.

Pancakes (using Baking Mix)

Yield: 10 to 12 medium pancakes

1 egg, beaten
⅓–½ cup water

1 cup Baking Mix (above)

Beat egg and water until light and fluffy. Add Baking Mix and stir just until ingredients are combined. Add additional Baking Mix or water if desired. Cook on hot griddle.

Biscuits (using Baking Mix)

Yield: 12 to 14 biscuits

2 cups Baking Mix (above)
¼ cup oil

¾–1 cup water

Preheat oven to 425°F. Combine ingredients. Stir with fork just until dough follows fork around bowl. Knead dough lightly on floured surface about 30 seconds or 10 times; too much handling makes biscuits tough. Roll or pat dough ½ inch thick. Cut into squares with pizza cutter and place on ungreased baking sheet. Bake for 10–12 minutes.

Corn Bread

Yield: 12 to 14 pieces

A tasty favorite that complements most any meal.

1 cup yellow cornmeal

1 cup whole wheat or white flour

1/3 cup sugar or honey

4 tsp. baking powder

1 tsp. salt

1 cup milk, or 1 cup water and 1/4 cup dry milk

1 large egg, beaten

1/3 cup oil

Preheat oven to 400°F. Mix cornmeal, flour, sugar, baking powder, and salt. If using dry milk, mix into dry ingredients. Combine milk or water, egg, and oil. Stir into flour mixture, mixing just until smooth. Pour into greased 9×9 or 8×12 pan, or fill greased muffin pans almost full, and bake. For corn bread, bake for 14–16 minutes. For muffins, bake for 12–15 min

Tip: To make fresh, nutritious, full-flavored cornmeal, mill popcorn in your grain mill on a medium coarse setting. Store, covered, in a cool dry place.

Banana Nut Bread

Yield: 1 (4x8) loaf or 3 (3x5) loaves

1 cup sugar or honey

1/3 cup oil

2 eggs

1 tsp. vanilla

3 large ripe bananas, mashed

1/4 cup water or milk

1 cup whole wheat flour

1 cup white flour

1 Tbsp. baking powder

1/2 tsp. baking soda

1/2 tsp. salt

1 tsp. cinnamon

1 tsp. pumpkin pie spice

1/2 cup chopped nuts

Preheat oven to 350°F. Beat sugar, oil, eggs, vanilla, mashed bananas, and water or milk until light and fluffy. Stir in flours, baking powder, baking soda, salt, and spices. Mix just until well blended. Stir in nuts. Pour into greased loaf pan or pans and bake for 35–40 minutes.

Apple Bread: Replace bananas with 2 medium apples, peeled, chopped, or shredded. Omit pumpkin pie spice.

Applesauce Bread

Yield: 1 (4x8) loaf or 3 (3x5) loaves

Applesauce Bread is a blue-ribbon winner.

1 cup brown or white sugar	2 tsp. baking powder
2 eggs, slightly beaten	½ tsp. baking soda
⅓ cup oil or shortening	½ tsp. salt
1 cup applesauce	1 tsp. cinnamon
¼ cup water	½ cup raisins
1 cup whole wheat flour or white flour	½ cup chopped nuts

Preheat oven to 350°F. Combine sugar, eggs, oil, applesauce, and water. Add flour, baking powder, baking soda, salt, and cinnamon. Mix just until moistened. Fold in raisins and nuts. Pour into greased loaf pans. Bake for 35–45 minutes.

Zucchini Bread

Yield: 2 medium loaves

This recipe makes tasty mini-muffins too.

1 cup sugar or honey	½ tsp. baking powder
½ cup oil	1 tsp. baking soda
2 eggs	1 tsp. salt
1 tsp. vanilla	2 tsp. cinnamon
2 cups grated zucchini	½ cup chopped nuts
1 cup whole wheat flour	1 cup raisins, optional
1½ cups white flour	

Preheat oven to 350°F. Beat sugar, oil, eggs, and vanilla until light and fluffy. Stir in zucchini. Add whole wheat and white flour, baking powder, baking soda, salt, and cinnamon. Mix until blended. Stir in nuts. Add raisins if desired. Pour batter into greased loaf pans and bake for 40–45 minutes.

Chocolate Zucchini Bread: Add 3 tablespoons of cocoa with dry ingredients. Sprinkle loaves with chocolate chips before baking.

Pumpkin Spice Bread

Yield: 3 loaves

Moist and delicious.

3 cups sugar

1 cup oil

4 eggs, slightly beaten

1 (15-oz.) can pumpkin

²/₃ cup water

4 cups flour

2 tsp. baking soda

1 tsp. baking powder

1 tsp. salt

1 Tbsp. pumpkin pie spice; or 2 tsp. cinnamon, 1 tsp. cloves, and ½ tsp. nutmeg

Preheat oven to 350°F. In large bowl, combine sugar, oil, eggs, pumpkin or cinnamon, and water. Add flour, baking soda, baking powder, salt, and pumpkin pie spice (or substitutes). Mix well. Pour into greased loaf pans and bake for 45–60 minutes.

Super Wheat Loaf (yeast-free)

Yield: 1 (4x8) loaf

Try it—you'll like it!

2½ cups whole wheat or white flour

½ cup sugar or honey

2 tsp. baking powder

1 tsp. baking soda

1 tsp. salt

pinch of cinnamon

¼ cup oil

1½ cups buttermilk, or 1⅓ cups water and ⅓ cup dry milk

1 Tbsp. vinegar

½ cup chopped nuts

Preheat oven to 350°F. Mix flour, sugar or honey, baking powder, baking soda, salt, and cinnamon. If using dry milk, mix into dry ingredients. Add oil, buttermilk or water, and vinegar and mix well. Stir in nuts. Pour into greased loaf pan. Let stand for 20 minutes before baking. Bake for 30–35 minutes.

Wheat Bread (yeast-free)

Yield: 1 (4x8) loaf

This tasty bread is great for sandwiches, toast, and so on.

1½ cups whole wheat flour
½ cup white flour
½ cup oats
2 Tbsp. sugar
1 Tbsp. baking powder

½ tsp. salt
½ cup sunflower seeds, optional
1 egg, beaten
1⅓ cups milk, or 1⅓ cups water and ⅓ cup dry milk

Preheat oven to 350°F. Combine flours, oats, sugar, baking powder, salt, and sunflower seeds (optional). If using dry milk, add to dry ingredients Mix egg and milk or water. Add to dry ingredients and stir just until well moistened. Pour into lightly greased loaf pans. Let stand for 20 minutes before baking. Bake for 35–40 minutes.

» FLAT BREADS

Pour-and-Cook Tortillas

Yield: 8 to 10 (6-inch) tortillas

1½ cups cold water
2 Tbsp. oil or 1 egg
½ cup cornmeal*

1 cup whole wheat or white flour
¼ tsp. salt

Put water, oil or egg, cornmeal, flour, and salt into blender. Jog and then blend until smooth. (No blender? Mix ingredients well using a wire whisk.) Pour batter onto a 400-degree griddle. Spread batter out to make thin rounds using the back of a spoon. Turn when edges look dry but not brown. Batter should be quite thin; add a small amount of water if too thick.

Tip: Cornmeal can be made by milling popcorn in your grain mill on a medium coarse setting.

Tortillas from Gloria

Yield: 10 to 12 tortillas

This recipe comes from an experienced cook who makes these daily for her family. Shortening is used traditionally and is best, but oil can be used.

2 cups white or whole wheat flour
½ tsp. salt
1 tsp. baking powder

3 Tbsp. shortening or oil
¾ cup very warm water

Mix flour, salt, and baking powder. Cut in shortening (if using oil instead, add with the water). Add warm water all at once, mixing with your fingers or in a bread mixer until dough forms a ball and isn't sticky. Knead for 2–3 minutes. Cover tightly with plastic wrap and let dough rest for 10–20 minutes. Pinch off golf ball–size pieces and form into balls. Keep dough covered at all times to prevent it from drying out. Roll out into very thin circles and cook on a nonstick griddle or in a dry cast-iron skillet at 400°F. Turn once.

Skillet Flat Bread

Yield: 3 (6-inch) rounds

This bread is good and easy.

1¼ cups flour
½ tsp. baking powder
¼ tsp. salt, plus more

3 Tbsp. oil or shortening, plus more
⅓ cup water

Combine flour, baking powder, and salt. Add oil or shortening and water. Mix with fork until dough forms. Knead for 1–2 minutes to form a ball. Cover tightly with plastic wrap and set aside for 30 minutes. Form dough into 3 balls. On lightly oiled surface, roll each ball of dough into a very thin 6-inch circle. Prick dough with fork, brush lightly with oil, and sprinkle with salt. Cook in hot nonstick skillet for 1–2 minutes each side or until flat bread is covered with golden-brown speckles. Stack between wax paper in warm oven. Cut into wedges with a pizza cutter or knife.

» YEAST BREADS

There's nothing like a loaf of bread or a pan of rolls golden and hot from the oven, ready to be spread with fresh butter and honey. This ancient homemaking skill has been brought up to date using new techniques—retaining its basic warmth, yet simplified by using modern methods to meet today's fast, busy pace.

The yeast bread and roll recipes in this book have all been streamlined for quick and easy preparation using "the quickmix method"—a time saver for the experienced cook and perfect for the novice because it gives consistently good results with a minimum of effort and mess.

Quickmix method: The dry yeast is mixed with some of the flour before adding any liquid. This eliminates the need to dissolve yeast first in warm water before starting to mix the dough. Quickmix makes it easier to blend ingredients, and there's no chance of lumps. The dough feels different when you are kneading it—lighter and springier than other dough. It rises faster because you can add warmer liquids (120°F–130°F) without killing the yeast, which has already been mixed with part of the flour. The warmer dough helps yeast work faster. Once you've used this method, you'll love the convenience, ease, and excellent results that it gives.

Conventional: If you prefer the conventional method, simply dissolve yeast in warm water (105°F–115°F) before adding it to the remaining ingredients.

Important: Bread stores best in a cool, dry place. It may be kept in the refrigerator but will dry and go stale more quickly. Bread keeps in the freezer at least three months if tightly wrapped. Slicing bread before freezing makes it convenient to use when only a slice or two is needed.

When milling wheat into flour: 2 cups whole wheat kernels makes about 3 cups flour.

Cup for cup, whole wheat and white flour are interchangeable.

Important: Before measuring any flour that has been sitting a while, fluff the flour up with a fork or measuring cup for a more accurate measurement.

Tip: The recipes below using dry milk are made with non-instant dry milk.

Nine Tips for Making Perfect Whole Wheat Bread

High-protein hard white wheat or hard red wheat makes the best bread because they contain the highest percentage of gluten. They also make good quick breads, pastries, and pasta.

#1 Start with Fresh Flour. When you mill your own wheat and use the flour immediately, you are assured of getting all the vitamins, minerals, bran, and fiber that nature intended. You reap the goodness of whole grains and none of the preservatives. Use the freshest flour available.

#2 Use Fresh yeast. Be sure yeast is active before you begin. See Proofing Yeast p. XX. Keep it active by using liquids at the proper temperature. Mix yeast and some of the flour before adding liquid. If you buy yeast in bulk, store it in a covered container in refrigerator or freezer after opening. Saf-Instant yeast is highly recommended for quality and shelf life.

#3 Use comfortably hot water. Water temperature is very important and should be 120°F–130°F if you add it to the flour/yeast mixture. Water that is too hot will kill yeast. If water is not warm enough, it will not fully activate the yeast. Warm water results in warm dough, which keeps the yeast active and helps the dough rise properly.

#4 Use the right amount of flour. Many factors affect the amount needed. If using a bread mixer, add the final few cups of flour one cup at a time while the machine is running. As the batter turns to dough, it clings together, creating an empty spot in the bowl. Add flour until dough begins to clean the sides of the bowl and pulls against itself as it kneads. The dough should hold its shape but still be a little sticky. Follow the same guide if making bread by hand. Be careful not to add too much flour, which is a common cause of heavy, dry bread.

#5 Develop the gluten. Gluten is the protein in wheat that gives structure and elasticity to batters and dough, and it is developed by thorough kneading. Using a bread mixer such as a Bosch is highly recommended. Sometimes called a "wife saver," it develops the gluten in minutes. This saves much time and effort and helps assure fine textured bread, especially when you're making whole wheat bread. Adding dry potato flakes, oats, applesauce, vital wheat gluten, lemon juice, ascorbic acid, and so on may also improve texture.

#6 A good breadmaker never has a failure, but instead learns to correct the inevitable, occasional mistake. If you should add too much flour, just drizzle a little warm water over the dough while mixing. It will soon return to the proper consistency. If dough seems too moist after kneading is complete, add a little white flour, usually ¼–½ cup, depending on the size of batch. Knead only until this flour blends in well, and shape dough immediately into loaves.

#7 Put a little oil or cooking spray on your hands and counter to prevent sticking as you mold the dough into loaves. Using flour to help shape the dough only makes for dry, crumbly bread. Besides, it gets all over you and the floor! Dough that is too dry can't rise properly. If desired, coat the dough with a light layer of oil after shaping, or cover with plastic wrap coated with cooking spray while it rises.

#8 Let the dough "proof" or rise. Always set a timer and keep a close eye on rising bread. In 20–30 minutes, the dough will double in size, depending on the temperature of the dough and the room. When dough has almost doubled in size, test for lightness by touching it lightly near the edge of the pan. A slight indentation should remain when it is ready for baking. If the indentation does not stay, let bread rise a few minutes more, which helps prevent heavy, compact bread. With a little practice, you'll know just when it is ready. If it gets too light, however, it may fall when baked.

#9 Preheat oven and bake until done. Place loaves carefully in the oven. In just 25–30 minutes, you'll have mouthwatering, fresh, crispy bread! Ovens vary, and your altitude may affect the baking time. You'll soon learn the right time and temperature for your oven.

The last step is always the best: Eat and enjoy!

How to Shape Loaves

Regular loaves: A loaf of bread can be formed in many ways, and most bakers have their favorites. Here are two simple methods that work well:

1. Using the palms of your hands, flatten the dough into a rectangle about 7×15 inches for a 4×8 loaf. Starting at the narrow side, roll dough up, sealing each turn tightly with the edge of your hand. Tuck in uneven ends. Roll dough back and forth to make it even. Place in a greased loaf pan. If dough is too long for the pan, lift up center, allowing the ends to fit, and then lay the center down. Dough will conform to the pan without remolding.

2. Hold a ball of dough in your hands. Keep tucking the edges of the dough underneath, turning the ball as you go until you have a smooth turtle's back shape. Gently elongate the ends until the dough resembles a football. Seal the edges underneath with your fingers. Place in a greased loaf pan.

Using the correctly sized bread pan is important. Too much or too little dough results in a poor loaf of bread, particularly when using whole wheat. Whole wheat dough is heavier than white dough and cannot support itself in a wide pan. For best results, bake whole grain bread in a 4×8 or narrower bread pan.

The following were calculated using 100 percent whole wheat bread dough.

Pan Size	Dough Weight	Cups of Dough
4×8	1½ pounds	3 cups
3×5	¾–1 pound	1½–2 cups

Perfect Whole Wheat Bread

This favorite recipe makes consistently good bread as well as light, crusty pan rolls, busy-day cinnamon rolls, pizza crust, and so on. (See tips on page 38, and variations starting on page 43.)

Large Batch

Yield: 5 to 6 (4x8) loaves

**14–16 cups whole wheat flour,
   or 12 cups whole wheat flour
   and 2–4 cups white flour**

**2 Tbsp. instant dry yeast,
   rounded**

6 cups warm water (125°F)

**¾–1 cup dry potato flakes or
   oats, optional**

½ cup sugar or honey

½ cup oil

1½ Tbsp. salt

Medium Batch

Yield: 4 (4x8) loaves

**10–12 cups whole wheat flour,
   or 8 cups whole wheat flour
   and 2–4 cups white flour**

2 Tbsp. instant dry yeast

4 cups warm water (125°F)

**⅓–½ cup dry potato flakes or
   oats, optional**

⅓ cup sugar or honey

⅓ cup oil

1 Tbsp. salt

Small Batch

Yield: 2 (4x8) loaves

**6–7 cups whole wheat flour,
   or 5 cups whole wheat flour
   and 1–2 cups white flour**

1 Tbsp. instant dry yeast

2 cups warm water (125°F)

**3 Tbsp. dry potato flakes or
   oats, optional**

3 Tbsp. sugar or honey

3 Tbsp. oil

2 tsp. salt

In mixer bowl equipped with kneading arm, combine 9, 6, or 3 cups flour (depending on desired batch size) and dry yeast. Add water, potato flakes or oats (optional), sugar or honey, oil, and salt. Mix well. If mixing by hand, cover and let batter sponge or rise for 10–15 minutes, which makes lighter bread with less kneading. Add remaining flour, 1 cup at a time, until dough forms a ball and cleans the sides of the bowl; the amount of flour needed may vary. Knead for 5–7 minutes by machine or 10–12 minutes by hand, until dough is smooth and elastic. Spray or oil counter. Divide dough into equal portions. Shape into loaves and place in greased bread pans. Cover with light cloth or plastic wrap sprayed lightly with cooking spray. Preheat oven to 350°F. Let dough rise until almost doubled. Bake until brown, 25–35 minutes. Remove loaves from pans, butter tops of loaves, and let cool on wire rack.

To improve bread texture if needed, use ONE of these additions. Adjust amount to fit your batch size.

½–1 cup applesauce

¼–½ tsp. ascorbic acid

1 cup buttermilk or yogurt in place of 1 cup water

vital wheat gluten, used as directed

dough enhancer, used as directed

Save time and mess! Make a large batch of dough, make bread, and use remaining dough to make some tasty variations:

Pan Rolls

For the dough, use the whole wheat recipe on page 42. Preheat oven to 350°F. Shape dough into a smooth ball. Using thumb and index finger as a pastry press, squeeze off uniform balls of dough. Tuck edges under to make smooth balls. Place rolls nearly touching in pan. Let rise until very light. Bake for 18–22 minutes.

Monkey Bread

For the dough, use the whole wheat recipe on page 42. Preheat oven to 350°F. Using your thumb and index finger as a pastry press, squeeze off walnut-sized balls of dough. Dip in melted butter, then roll in a cinnamon/sugar mix made from 1 tablespoon cinnamon and ½ cup sugar. Place balls in layers in a greased bread pan or tube pan. Let rise until light. Bake for 20–30 minutes (depending on the number of layers in the pan). Serve warm.

Busy-Day Cinnamon Rolls

Yield: 15 cinnamon rolls

For the dough, use the whole wheat recipe on page 42. Preheat oven to 350°F. Roll out 3 cups of dough into a 10×16 rectangle. Brush with soft butter and sprinkle with a cinnamon/sugar mix made from 1 tablespoon cinnamon and ½ cup sugar. Sprinkle with ½ cup raisins. Roll up tightly and pinch edges to seal. Cut into 15 (1-inch) slices using a piece of dental floss or string. Place rolls 3 across and 5 down in greased 9×13 baking dish. Flatten slightly with palm of hand. Let rise till double. Bake for 16–18 minutes. Don't overbake. Drizzle glaze (see below) over warm cinnamon rolls.

Glaze: 2 Tbsp. hot water, ½ tsp. vanilla, and 1 cup powdered sugar. Whisk water and vanilla into powdered sugar.

Pizza Crust

For the dough, use the whole wheat recipe on page 42. Preheat oven to 450°F. Use a pizza roller to roll 1½-2½ cups of dough about ¼ inch thick on a greased pizza pan or baking sheet (amount of dough will vary according to pan size and desired thickness of crust). Make a thin, crispy crust or thick, chewy crust. Add sauce and toppings. Bake for 6–8 minutes (small or medium pizza) or 10 minutes (large).

OSM Bread

Yield: 3 (4x8) loaves

This light gourmet bread is a real tasty treat.

5 cups whole wheat flour
2 Tbsp. instant dry yeast
1/3 cup sugar or honey
3 cups warm water (125°F)
1/3 cup oil
2 tsp. salt

1/2 cup oats
1/2 cup sunflower seeds
1/4 cup millet
2–3 cups white or whole wheat flour

Preheat oven to 350°F. Mix 5 cups whole wheat flour, dry yeast, and sugar in mixing bowl (equipped with kneading arm if mixing by machine). Add water, oil, and salt (if using honey, add with water and oil) and mix well. Mix in oats, sunflower seeds, and millet. If mixing by hand, cover and let batter sponge or rise for 12–15 minutes, which makes lighter bread with less kneading. Add white or whole wheat flour 1/2 cup at a time until dough forms a ball and cleans the sides of the bowl. Dough should be moist but not sticky, firm but not dry. Knead for 5–6 minutes by machine (or 10–12 minutes by hand). Divide dough into equal portions. Shape into loaves and place in greased bread pans. Cover with plastic wrap sprayed lightly with cooking spray. Let rise until doubled. Bake for 35 minutes. Remove from pans, butter tops, and let cool on wire rack.

Potato Bread

Yield: 5 (4x8) loaves

This is a very fine-textured light bread.

10–12 cups whole wheat flour, divided

2 Tbsp. instant dry yeast, rounded

½ cup dry potato flakes

⅓ cup sugar or honey

5 cups warm water (125°F)

⅓ cup oil

1 Tbsp. salt

2 cups white flour

Preheat oven to 350°F. Combine 6 cups whole wheat flour, dry yeast, potato flakes, and sugar or honey in mixing bowl. Add water and oil and mix well. If mixing by hand, cover and let batter rise for 12–15 minutes, which makes lighter bread with less kneading. Mix in salt and white flour. Add remaining whole wheat flour 1 cup at a time until batter forms a ball and cleans the sides of the bowl. Knead for 5–6 minutes by machine or 10 minutes by hand. Divide dough into 5 equal portions and shape into loaves. Place in greased bread pans. Cover with damp cloth if desired. Let rise until almost doubled and bake for 30–35 minutes. Remove from pans, butter tops, and cool on rack.

Oatmeal Bread

Yield: 2 (4x8) loaves

Moist and satisfying, this bread requires very little kneading.

1 cup oats
2 cups hot water (125°F)
⅓ cup oil
⅓ cup molasses or honey
3 cups whole wheat flour

2 Tbsp. instant dry yeast
2 tsp. salt
1–2 cups white flour
water and oatmeal (optional)

Preheat oven to 350°F. In large bowl, combine oats, hot water, oil, and molasses or honey. Let cool for 5–7 minutes. Add whole wheat flour and dry yeast and mix thoroughly. Cover and let stand about 15 minutes. Add salt and white flour, 1 cup at a time, until dough begins to clean sides of bowl. Dough should be a little sticky but manageable. Knead for 4–6 minutes. Shape into 2 loaves and place in greased bread pans. If desired, brush loaves with water and sprinkle with a little oatmeal. Let rise till doubled and bake until brown, 25–35 minutes.

Pioneer Wheat Bread

Yield: 2 (4x8) loaves

Make this tasty bread by hand. Children love to help.

6 cups whole wheat flour, divided

1 Tbsp. instant dry yeast

⅓ cup dry milk

3 cups warm water (125°F)

1 Tbsp. oil

1 Tbsp. honey

1 Tbsp. molasses

1 Tbsp. salt

Preheat oven to 350°F. Combine 4 cups flour, dry yeast, and dry milk. Add water, oil, honey, and molasses and mix well. For lighter bread with less kneading, cover and let mixture sponge or rise for 12–15 minutes. Add salt and remaining flour, 1 cup at a time, until dough begins to clean sides of the bowl; dough should not be too stiff. Knead for about 6 minutes or until dough is smooth and satiny. Allow dough to rest for 10 minutes, then shape into 2 loaves. Place in greased bread pans and let rise until almost doubled. Bake until golden, 30 minutes. Remove from pans and cool on rack.

Light Whole Wheat Bread

Yield: 5 to 6 loaves

Rich and delicious.

5 cups warm water (125°F)

2/3 cup oil

2/3 cup honey or sugar

2–3 Tbsp. instant dry yeast

½ cup high-gluten flour or oats

11–12 cups whole wheat flour, or 8 cups whole wheat flour and 3–4 cups white flour

Place water in mixing bowl. Stir in oil, honey or sugar, and yeast. Let stand for 5 minutes to let yeast soften. Add gluten flour and 7 cups flour to the liquid and mix for 2–3 minutes. Gradually add remainder of the flour until dough cleans sides of the bowl. Knead for 5–7 minutes, until smooth and satiny. Place a small amount of oil on countertop. Turn out dough (it will be a little sticky) and shape into the size and number of loaves desired. Place in greased pans; cover with damp cloth and let rise until almost doubled. Place in cold oven and turn oven to 350°F. Bake for 30–35 minutes. Remove from pans, butter tops of loaves, and cool on wire racks.

White Bread

Yield: 4 to 5 (4x8) loaves

Velvety texture with a tender crust. This recipe adapts easily to half white and half whole wheat flour.

11–12 cups white flour, or half white flour and half whole wheat flour

2 Tbsp. instant dry yeast

¼ cup sugar

1 (12-oz.) can evaporated milk

3 cups warm water (125°F)

¼ cup oil

1 Tbsp. salt

Preheat oven to 350°F. Mix 6 cups flour, dry yeast, and sugar in bowl. Add evaporated milk and then warm water, oil, and salt. Mix well. If mixing by hand, cover and let this batter sponge or rise for 10–15 minutes. Mix, adding remaining flour 1 cup at a time, until dough just cleans sides of the bowl. Knead for 3–5 minutes by machine or about 10 minutes by hand. Stop mixing, cover bowl, and let dough rise to top of bowl, 15–20 minutes. Knead dough down. Lightly oil hands and divide dough into equal portions. Shape into loaves and place in greased bread pans. Cover with plastic wrap sprayed lightly with cooking spray. Let rise until doubled and bake for 25–35 minutes. Remove from pans, butter tops, and let cool on wire rack.

White Bread by Hand

Yield: 2 (4x8) loaves

This easy recipe can also be made using a machine.

5–6 cups white flour, divided
1 Tbsp. instant dry yeast
2 Tbsp. sugar

2 cups warm water (125°F)
2 Tbsp. oil
2 tsp. salt

Preheat oven to 350°F. Mix 3 cups flour, yeast, and sugar. Add water, oil, and salt and mix well. Cover and let batter sponge or rise for about 10 minutes. Add remaining flour, 1 cup at a time, mixing it in with a hand mixer or stirring with a spoon. Continue to add flour until dough is too stiff to stir. Pour dough onto a floured surface and knead dough, adding flour until the dough is no longer sticky but is elastic and smooth, about 10 minutes. Put a small amount of oil in the mixing bowl and add dough ball, turning to coat all sides with oil. Cover with damp cloth and let rise until almost doubled. Punch down. Divide dough into 2 pieces. Shape each into a loaf and place in greased bread pans, making sure top of bread is smooth. Cover with plastic wrap sprayed lightly with cooking spray. Let dough rise until doubled in size. Bake until golden, 25–35 minutes. Remove from pans, butter tops, and cool on wire rack.

French Bread

Yield: 1 large loaf

French Bread is crusty, delicious, and easy to make.

3–4 cups whole wheat or white flour, divided

1 Tbsp. instant dry yeast

1 Tbsp. sugar

1 cup warm water (125°F)

3 Tbsp. oil

1 tsp. salt

Preheat oven to 375°F. Combine 2 cups flour, dry yeast, and sugar in bowl. Add water, oil, and salt and mix well. If mixing by hand, cover and let batter sponge or rise for 10–15 minutes. Add remaining flour ½ cup at a time until batter forms a ball and cleans sides of mixing bowl. Dough should be quite stiff. Knead for 4–5 minutes by machine or 8–10 minutes by hand, or until dough is smooth and elastic. Lightly oil hands and countertop. Roll dough into a 10×15 rectangle. Roll up tightly, beginning with the wide side. Seal edges by pinching them together and then taper ends. Place loaf seam side down on a lightly greased baking sheet. Diagonally slash loaf ¼ inch deep every 2 inches across the top. Brush with water. Let rise uncovered until doubled. Bake until top is deep golden brown, 25–30 minutes.

Hard Rolls

Preheat oven to 375°F. Make French Bread dough (p. XX). Shape dough into small oval rolls. Place on lightly greased baking sheets. Let rise until doubled. Bake for 15–18 minutes.

Batter Bread

Yield: 2 small loaves

This open-textured bread requires no kneading.

3 cups white or whole wheat flour

1 Tbsp. instant dry yeast

2 Tbsp. sugar

1 tsp. salt

1½ cups warm water (125°F)

2 Tbsp. oil

Preheat oven to 350°F. Combine flour, dry yeast, sugar, and salt. Add warm water and oil and mix well for 3–5 minutes. Cover dough and let rise until doubled, 25–30 minutes. Stir down batter by beating about 25 strokes with a large wooden spoon. Pour batter into 2 greased loaf pans. Smooth top of dough by patting into shape with oiled hands. Let rise until doubled. Bake until golden, 25–35 minutes. Remove from pans, butter tops, and cool on rack.

Sourdough Starter

A good beginning for country breads.

2 cups white or whole wheat flour

1 Tbsp. instant dry yeast

1 Tbsp. sugar or honey

2 cups warm water (125°F)

Combine flour, dry yeast, and sugar or honey in bowl. Stir in warm water and beat until smooth. Cover with plastic wrap. Let sit in warm place for 2 days. Stir 2–3 times each day. Always save at least 1 cup to keep the starter going.

To use in recipe: Measure out amount called for in recipe and use as directed.

To replenish starter: Stir in 2 cups warm water and 2 cups flour. Store covered in warm place for at least 5 hours. Cover and store in refrigerator. Stir before using. Never add anything to starter but the flour and water needed to keep it going. If not used in one week, remove 2 cups starter and follow directions for replenishing.

Sourdough Bread

Yield: 3 loaves

This bread is the real deal.

5–6 cups white or whole wheat flour, divided
1 Tbsp. instant dry yeast
3 Tbsp. sugar
½ tsp. baking soda

1 tsp. salt
1 cup warm water (125°F)
1½ cups sourdough starter (p. XX)
2 Tbsp. oil

Preheat oven to 400°F. Combine 2 cups flour, dry yeast, sugar, baking soda, and salt. Add water and mix well. Add starter and oil and beat until smooth. Mix in remaining flour, 1 cup at a time, to make a medium stiff dough. Knead for 6–8 minutes, until smooth and elastic. Or if making by hand, place in greased bowl, turning bowl to grease top. Cover and let rise in warm place until doubled. Punch dough down. Divide dough into 3 equal pieces. Form each into a smooth round ball or a 14-inch tapered roll. Place on greased baking sheets. With a sharp knife, make several cuts in a crisscross fashion on tops of round loaves or several diagonal cuts on tops of long loaves. Let rise until doubled and bake for 25–30 minutes.

Sourdough Biscuits

Yield: 12 biscuits

These biscuits are light and fluffy with a marvelous tangy taste.

1½ cups flour
2 tsp. baking powder
½ tsp. baking soda

½ tsp. salt
¼ cup oil
1 cup sourdough starter (p. XX)

Preheat oven to 400°F. Mix flour, baking powder, baking soda, and salt. Stir in oil and starter. Knead lightly until smooth and satiny. Pinch off dough to form balls. Dip in melted butter or oil. Place dough balls in greased 9-inch square baking dish. Let rise until doubled. Bake for 15–18 minutes.

Sourdough Hotcakes

Yield: 12 to 15 hotcakes

Serve with butter and lots of syrup!

½ cup sourdough starter (p. XX)

1 cup flour

1 cup milk, or 1 cup water and ¼ cup dry milk

2 Tbsp. sugar

½ tsp. salt

1 egg, slightly beaten

2 Tbsp. oil

1 tsp. baking soda

Mix starter, flour, milk, sugar, and salt in bowl. Let sit covered in warm place overnight. If using dry milk, add to dry ingredients. Just before using, remove 1 cup batter to replenish starter. To the remaining batter in the bowl, add egg, oil, and baking soda. Mix well. For thinner hotcakes, add more milk or water. Cook hotcakes on 375-degree griddle. Serve with butter and syrup or honey.

» ROLLS AND BUNS

How to shape rolls and buns:

Work on a lightly oiled surface. Preheat oven to 350°F.

Pan rolls: Shape dough into a large, smooth ball. Using thumb and index finger as a pastry press, squeeze off uniform 1- to 2-inch balls of dough. Tuck edges under or roll to make smooth balls. Dip into melted butter if desired. Place on greased pan, letting balls just barely touch each other. Let rise until very light, at least doubled in size. Bake in preheated oven until crusty brown, 18–22 minutes.

Quick Parker House rolls: Roll dough into a ⅜-inch-thick rectangle and brush lightly with soft butter. Cut dough into 2×2½ rectangles with pizza cutter. Pick up each piece and stretch slightly to thin dough in the middle. Fold off-center so top half overlaps the bottom and firmly press folded edge. Place almost touching on greased baking sheet. Let rise until doubled and bake in preheated oven for 18–20 minutes.

Hoagie buns: Roll dough into a rectangle ½-inch thick. Use a pizza cutter and cut into strips 2–3 inches wide and 6 inches long, or any desired size. Dough may also be molded into oblong rolls. Place on a greased baking sheet. Let rise for 12–20 minutes and then bake in preheated oven for 15–20 minutes.

Hamburger buns: Roll dough ⅜ inch thick. Cut into rounds using a quart can or other large cutter. Place on greased baking sheet. Let rise for 12–20 minutes and then bake for 16–18 minutes.

Hot dog buns: Roll dough ¾ inch thick. Cut into 2×5 strips, or bend an empty quart can into an oval and use as a dough cutter. Place dough on greased baking sheet. Let rise for 12–20 minutes and then bake in preheated oven for 15–18 minutes.

Feather Rolls

Yield: 60 large rolls

6 cups whole wheat flour, divided

3 Tbsp. instant dry yeast

2/3 cup sugar or honey

3 cups warm water (125°F)

2/3 cup oil

4 large eggs

4 tsp. salt

3–4 cups white flour

Preheat oven to 350°F. In large bowl, mix 4 cups whole wheat flour, yeast, and sugar or honey. Add water, oil, and eggs. Mix well for 2–3 minutes. Add salt and remaining 2 cups whole wheat flour and mix well. Add white flour 1 cup at a time until dough begins to clean the sides of the bowl. Knead for 5–7 minutes. Dough should be very soft and manageable. If dough stiffens while mixing, drizzle a little warm water over dough as it kneads. If kneading by hand, cover dough and let rise until doubled. Lightly oil hands and countertop. Shape into dinner rolls or cinnamon rolls. Let rise until very light. Bake until golden brown, 18–22 minutes.

Wheat 'n' White Rolls

Yield: 7- to 8-dozen rolls

This is a delicious large roll or cinnamon roll recipe.

5 cups whole wheat flour

4 Tbsp. instant dry yeast

500 mg vitamin C, crushed (optional)

2/3 cup brown sugar or honey

1 Tbsp. salt

5 cups warm water (125°F)

2/3 cup oil

4 eggs

8–10 cups white flour

Preheat oven to 350°F. Mix whole wheat flour, dry yeast, vitamin C, brown sugar, and salt in mixer bowl. Add water, oil, and eggs and mix well. Add enough white flour to make dough pull away from the sides of the bowl. The dough should be sticky but manageable. Knead for 6–7 minutes. Cover bowl and let rise until doubled. Shape as desired. Let rise until doubled. Bake until golden brown, 16–18 minutes. If you're making cinnamon rolls, frost with Caramel Frosting (p. XX) or Cinnamon Roll Glaze (p. XX).

Cinnamon Rolls

Yield: 15 cinnamon rolls

The apple filling is scrumptious. The rolls are tender too.

4 cups whole wheat flour	**⅓ cup oil**
2 Tbsp. instant dry yeast	**2 eggs**
2 cups warm water (125°F)	**2 tsp. salt**
⅓ cup sugar or honey	**1–2 cups whole wheat or white flour**

Preheat oven to 350°F. In mixer bowl, combine 4 cups flour and dry yeast. Add water, sugar or honey, oil, eggs, and salt. Mix well. Add remaining flour, ½ cup at a time, until dough begins to clean sides of the bowl. Do not add too much flour. Dough should be soft and manageable. Knead for 5–6 minutes. On lightly oiled surface, roll half the dough into a 16×8 rectangle about ¼ inch thick. Cover with desired filling (see below). Roll up tightly, beginning at the wide side. Seal the seam well by pinching edges of dough together. With seam side down, cut dough into 1-inch slices using dental floss or string. Place rolls 3 across and 5 down on greased baking sheet. Cover lightly with plastic wrap and let rise until very light and doubled in size. Bake until golden, 16–18 minutes. Let cool slightly. Drizzle Cinnamon Roll Glaze (p. XX) over warm rolls or frost with Caramel Frosting (p. XX). Repeat with other half of dough if desired, or make into dinner rolls.

Apple Filling

soft butter	**½ cup raisins**
applesauce	**¼ cup sugar**
1 apple, shredded	**2 tsp. cinnamon**

Brush dough rectangle (p. XX) lightly with soft butter. Spread evenly with applesauce, shredded apples, raisins, sugar, and cinnamon

Cinnamon-Butter Filling

3–4 Tbsp. soft butter
½ cup sugar
1 Tbsp. cinnamon

½ cup raisins
½ cup chopped nuts, optional

Spread soft butter over dough rectangle. Mix sugar and cinnamon and spread evenly over dough. Sprinkle with raisins and nuts, as desired.

Cinnamon Roll Glaze

2 cups powdered sugar
¼ cup hot water

1 tsp. vanilla
dash of salt

Whisk powdered sugar into hot water, vanilla, and salt. Drizzle glaze over warm cinnamon rolls.

Caramel Frosting

So yummy on cinnamon rolls, cakes, and so on.

⅓ cup butter
1 cup brown sugar
⅓ cup water

1 tsp. vanilla
pinch of salt
2–3 cups powdered sugar

Heat butter, brown sugar, and water until bubbly. Cool, then add vanilla, salt, and powdered sugar until frosting reaches desired consistency. Mix until smooth, creamy, and easy to spread.

Batter Rolls

Yield: 24 rolls

3–4 cups whole wheat or white
    flour, divided

1 Tbsp. instant dry yeast

¼ cup sugar or honey

1½ cups warm water (125°F)

⅓ cup oil

1 egg, beaten

½ tsp. vanilla

1 tsp. salt

Preheat oven to 350°F. Mix 2 cups flour, dry yeast, and sugar in mixing bowl. Stir in warm water. Add oil, egg, vanilla, and salt and mix well. Add remaining flour ½ cup at a time to form medium-thick batter. Mix until smooth. Cover and let rise until doubled. Punch dough down. Drop dough in well-greased muffin tins and let rise until doubled. Bake until golden brown, 20–22 minutes. Remove from pans and serve immediately.

Breadsticks

Yield: 18 breadsticks

3 Tbsp. butter

3–4 cups whole wheat or white
    flour, divided

1 Tbsp. instant dry yeast

2 Tbsp. sugar

1 tsp. salt

1½ cups warm water (125°F)

parmesan cheese

garlic salt

Preheat oven to 375°F. Melt butter in 9×13 baking dish while oven is preheating. When butter is melted, remove dish from oven and spread butter evenly to cover bottom. In bowl, mix 2 cups flour, dry yeast, sugar, and salt. Add water and mix well. Add remaining flour ½ cup at a time to make medium-soft dough. Knead for 3–4 minutes. Put dough into baking dish and roll with pizza roller or pat with hands to fit dish. Turn dough over once to coat with butter. Sprinkle with parmesan cheese and garlic salt. With pizza cutter, cut dough horizontally into nine 1×13 strips, alternating directions of pizza cutter each row to keep dough from creeping. Next, cut dough across the middle to make 18 breadsticks. Let rise for 15–20 minutes, or until almost doubled. Bake for 18–20 minutes.

CHAPTER 3

Gluten-Free Is Here to Stay

» Gluten-Free Cooking and Baking

Today, many people are sensitive to foods containing gluten. Eating healthy without gluten is easier than you think. Focus on foods that are naturally gluten-free such as fruits, vegetables, beans, legumes, seeds, nuts, low-fat dairy, fish, and lean meats. Remember to drink lots of water to help your body process all that good fiber.

There are more than one hundred fifty delicious gluten-free, nutrient-dense recipes in this book, so enjoy! Included here are recipes for gluten-free pancakes and a yeast-free, gluten-free bread that doesn't include xanthan gum or guar gum. The pancake and waffle recipes can also be used for bread if necessary. Make sure the bouillon, soy sauce, or spices you use are all gluten-free. Knox or other unflavored gelatin may be used in place of xanthan gum or guar gum. Gelatin does not cause the digestive upsets frequently reported from using gums in recipes, plus it is much less expensive and is easy to find in most grocery stores.

» Gluten-Free Food Storage Ideas

Prepare now for the unexpected. Make sure you have a supply of gluten-free flour on hand. Have a seventy-two-hour kit or, better yet, a two-week supply of gluten-free foods that would provide adequate calories and protein in the event of an emergency. Keep gluten-free flour in the freezer or the ingredients to make gluten-free flour in your pantry. Consider storing brown rice, dry beans, lentils, and other nutrient-dense, gluten-free foods. Eat them on a regular basis so your body is used to digesting them. Gluten-free pasta and

sauce, gluten-free chili, canned fruits and vegetables, and canned chicken and other meats are good to have in storage. Read labels to ensure the foods are gluten-free. Rotate on a regular basis to maintain freshness.

» Gluten-Free Cream Soups

To replace condensed soups, use our easy Gluten-Free Cream Soup Mix (p. XX). This works well and can be used in a variety of recipes. Make sure the bouillon granules are gluten-free.

» Gluten-Free Oats

When making oat flour, make sure the oats are certified gluten-free. This certification assures the oats have been grown and processed in a wheat-free environment. Check with your doctor first to see if you can tolerate oats.

» Gluten-Free Flour Mixes

Commercial gluten-free flour or baking mixes may be used in any of the baking recipes containing flour in this book. Be aware that gluten-free flours are *not* all nutritionally equal. Many gluten-free mixes are made from white rice flour and sweet rice flour, which are low in nutrients and fiber, so check the ingredient list carefully. Look for brown rice flour, sorghum, millet, almond meal, and flax meal. These flours are more nutritious and contain fiber.

Superfine Brown Rice Flour

Adjust grain mill to finest setting before milling brown rice. Use this mill for gluten-free grains only. Milling brown rice assures fresh nutritious flour and saves money as well. A good gluten-free flour mix recipe is listed below.

Authenticfoods.com has superfine brown rice flour. It is powdery and fine, eliminating the gummy texture in baked goods, and can be ordered directly online.

GF Whole Grain Flour Blend

Yield: 6 cups mix

4 cups superfine brown rice flour (available at authentic-foods.com and some health food stores, or make your own as directed on p. XX)

1⅓ cups potato starch (*not* potato flour) or cornstarch

⅔ cups tapioca starch/flour

Whisk ingredients together so there are no "trails" of unmixed flour and starch. Store the flour blend in a tightly covered container in the pantry or freezer.

Whole Grain Gluten-Free Flours

- Brown rice flour
- Buckwheat flour
- Corn flour
- Mesquite flour
- Millet flour
- Oat flour
- Quinoa flour
- Sorghum flour
- Sweet potato flour
- Teff flour

White Gluten-Free Flours/Starches

- Arrowroot flour
- Cornstarch
- Potato flour
- Potato starch
- Sweet rice flour
- Tapioca flour
- White rice flour

Nut Flours

- Almond flour
- Chestnut flour
- Coconut flour
- Hazelnut flour

SOME NOTES:

- Many of the breakfast recipes and most of the lunch and dinner recipes in this book are gluten-free. Any recipe not calling for a gluten-containing grain can be considered gluten-free as long as the guidelines below are followed.

- Any gluten-free flour mix can be substituted for many of the quick bread recipes in this book. Substitute gluten-free flour mix cup for cup with regular flour.

- Make sure bouillon and all spices are gluten-free. Read the labels.

- Check labels on canned chili, spaghetti sauce, tomato sauce, and barbecue sauce to make sure they are gluten-free.

- Use gluten-free noodles.

- Make sure mayonnaise and salad dressings are gluten-free—read the label.

- If a recipe calls for cream soup, use the gluten-free cream soup in this book (p. XX).

- Keep the nutrition factor in mind when selecting gluten-free products. Pamelasproducts.com has nutritional gluten-free flour and baking mixes available. You can subscribe to them on amazon.com and have the products delivered to your door at a specified interval, making gluten-free baking much easier. Pamela's products are also available in many health food stores and grocery stores.

GF Yeast-Free Bread

Yield: 1 (4x8) loaf or 2 (3x5) loaves

This bread is great for sandwiches, toast, and French toast.

1½ cups superfine brown rice flour

½ cup tapioca starch

2 Tbsp. sugar

½ tsp. baking soda

1½ tsp. baking powder

1 tsp. salt

1 egg

1 cup buttermilk or 1 Tbsp. vinegar in 1 cup water

Preheat oven to 350°F. Combine rice flour, tapioca starch, sugar, baking soda, baking powder, and salt in mixing bowl. Whisk dry ingredients together until well mixed. In mixing up, whisk together egg and buttermilk, or water and vinegar. Add to dry ingredients, stirring until well combined. Immediately pour into greased 4 x 8 pan. Bake until toothpick inserted in center comes out clean, 25–30 minutes. Don't overbake. Cool on a wire rack for 10 minutes before removing from pan.

Tip: To make oat flour, Blend quick or regular oats in blender until fine.

Note: If you are sensitive to gluten-free oats, Superfine Brown Rice Flour (p. XX) may be used for all of the flour. Or, you may use your favorite gluten-free flour for the first 3 ingredients. If your flour blend contains sugar, salt, soda, and baking powder, don't add these ingredients as listed in the recipe.

GF Corn Bread

Yield: 9 to 12

Moist and delicious.

1 cup cornmeal
1 cup gluten-free flour mix
½ tsp. unflavored gelatin
¼ cup sugar
1 tsp. salt
2 tsp. baking powder

1 tsp. soda
1 cup applesauce
2 eggs, well beaten
¼ cup oil
2 Tbsp. water

Preheat oven to 350°F. Mix cornmeal, gluten-free flour mix, gelatin, sugar, salt, baking powder, and baking soda. Add applesauce, eggs, oil, and water. Stir until well combined. Pour into greased 8×8 or 8×12 pan. Bake until golden brown, or until inserted toothpick comes out clean, 18–20 minutes. Don't overbake.

GF Oatmeal Pancakes or Waffles

Yield: 15 to 20 pancakes

2 cups oat flour*
2 Tbsp. sugar
1 Tbsp. baking powder
1 Tbsp. cornstarch

½ tsp. salt
2 eggs, well beaten
1 Tbsp. oil
1¼–1½ cups milk or water

Combine oat flour, sugar, baking powder, cornstarch, and salt. Whisk in eggs, oil, and milk or water. Mix just until dry ingredients are well moistened. Thin with water if needed. Make pancakes or waffles. The pancakes or waffles may also be used as bread for sandwiches.

Tip: To make oat flour, blend quick or regular oats in blender until fine.

GF Whole Grain Quick Mix (like Bisquick)

**1 recipe gluten-free flour blend
(6 cups)**

**¼ cup flaxseed meal or almond
meal or protein powder**

**1 Tbsp. xanthan gum or
1 packet Knox unflavored
gelatin**

2 tsp. salt

¼ cup baking powder

1½ cups shortening

Whisk dry ingredients together. Cut in shortening until mix is the size of small peas. Store the quick mix in airtight container in refrigerator or cool pantry.

GF Quick Mix Pancakes or Waffles

Yield: 12 (2-inch) pancakes

**1 cup GF Whole Grain Quick Mix
(see previous recipe)**

1 Tbsp. sugar

1 egg, slightly beaten

⅓–½ cup milk, any kind

Whisk ingredients together. Cook on hot griddle or waffle iron. Pancakes and waffles can be used as sandwich bread.

GF Quick Mix Muffins

Yield: 12 muffins

**1½ cups GF Whole Grain Quick
Mix (see above)**

2 Tbsp. sugar

1 Tbsp. dry milk

½ cup water

1 egg, beaten

2 Tbsp. oil

Preheat oven to 350°F. In bowl, combine quick mix, sugar, and dry milk. Add water, egg, and oil. Mix just until well blended. Fill paper-lined muffin tins ⅓ to ½ full. Bake for 12–15 minutes. Don't overbake or muffins will be dry.

Note: For chocolate muffins, increase sugar to 4 tablespoons and add 2–3 tablespoons chocolate syrup. Bake as directed above.

GF Banana Bread

Yield: 2 medium loaves or 4 (3x5) loaves

A real tasty treat.

¾ cup sugar

⅓ cup oil

2 eggs

1½ cups mashed banana (2–3 bananas)

⅓ cup water

1 cup brown rice flour

¾ cup millet flour

1 tsp. baking soda

½ tsp. salt

¼ tsp. baking powder

½ tsp. xanthan gum or Knox unflavored gelatin

½ cup chopped walnuts, optional

Preheat oven to 350°F. Beat sugar, oil, and eggs until mixture is thoroughly combined. Mix in banana and water. Add flours, baking soda, salt, baking powder, and xanthan gum or gelatin. Mix just until blended. Add nuts if desired. Pour batter into greased pans and bake for 30–35 minutes.

GF Peanut Butter Cookies

Yield: 16 to 18 (2-inch) cookies

No one can tell these are gluten-free.

1 cup peanut butter or other nut butter

½ cup sugar

1 egg

1 tsp. vanilla

granulated sugar, optional

Preheat oven to 350°F. Mix ingredients well. Shape dough into 1-inch balls. Roll in granulated sugar if desired. Place on baking sheet. Crisscross each cookie with fork to flatten. Bake for 15–18 minutes.

GF Chocolate Chip Cookies

Yield: 20 (2-inch) cookies

Crisp and yummy.

¼ cup vegetable shortening	1¼ cups gluten-free flour
¼ cup sugar	½ tsp. salt
½ cup brown sugar	1 tsp. baking powder
1 egg	½ tsp. baking soda
1 tsp. vanilla	½ cup chocolate chips

Preheat oven to 350°F. In bowl, cream shortening, sugars, egg, and vanilla until fluffy. In another bowl, mix flour, salt, baking powder, and baking soda. Add dry ingredients to shortening mix, and mix well. Stir in chocolate chips. Drop dough by tablespoonfuls 2 inches apart on greased or sprayed baking sheet. Bake just until edges are light brown, 8–10 minutes. Don't overbake. Let cool on baking sheet for 10 minutes before moving to cooling rack.

GF Black Bean Brownies

Yield: 16 brownies

Rich and moist!

1 (14-oz.) can black beans; drained, rinsed well, and finely mashed

3 eggs

2 Tbsp. oil

1 cup sugar

½ cup cocoa

1 tsp. vanilla

½ tsp. baking powder

½ tsp. salt

¼ cup gluten-free chocolate chips

Preheat oven to 350°F. In mixer, place finely mashed black beans, eggs, oil, sugar, cocoa, vanilla, baking powder, and salt. Mix until smooth. Pour batter into 8×8 greased pan and sprinkle with the chocolate chips. Bake until a toothpick inserted in the center comes out clean and edges start to pull away from the sides of the pan, 40–45 minutes. Watch closely and don't overbake.

Tip: If using a glass pan, reduce the temperature to 325°F.

CHAPTER 4

Breakfast Favorites

When you eat a nourishing breakfast, you have more energy, stamina, and mental alertness all day. Children who eat a good breakfast do better in school. Learn to eat for how you want to look and feel. Whole grains make a good start for many folks.

Delicious, healthy smoothies are also a good choice for breakfast, especially when you don't have time to sit down and eat. Smoothies make a nourishing and refreshing drink, not only for breakfast but also for an energizing afternoon snack. Power-loading smoothies with vegetables can accelerate weight loss, detoxify the body, and build health in general.

The best part about making smoothies is that every recipe is adaptable to your personal taste and what you may have on hand. This will probably vary with the seasons, and variety is good for health. If needed, smoothies can be part of a progressive breakfast. Add some bran muffins and eat on the run. Experiment a bit and you'll soon find your favorite combinations.

This chapter has recipes for everything from smoothies to cereals to pancakes. Enjoy!

» Favorite Smoothie Ideas

The following list gives suggested ingredients that can be included in your smoothies. Pick and choose ingredients as desired. Use fresh or frozen fruit and vegetables. Vary amounts to suit your taste and what you have on hand. Bananas complement any combination. Adding oats thickens smoothies and adds nutrition and satiety.

Make smoothies as simple or as full-bodied as desired.

water or fruit juice, etc.

yogurt, any flavor

protein powder

raw almonds

golden flaxseed or flaxseed meal

greens: spinach, kale, spring mix, etc.

celery, cut in 2-inch pieces

carrot, peeled and cut

ripe avocado

medium beet, peeled and cut

sprouted wheat, sunflower seeds, etc.

oats

honey or agave

apple, pear, peach, orange, etc.; quartered

frozen* or fresh bananas, cut

fresh, frozen, or canned pineapple

frozen berry mix

frozen fruit mix

Put water or juice, yogurt, protein powder, almonds, and flaxseed in blender and mix. Add greens, celery, carrot, avocado, and beet and blend well. Add wheat, oats, and honey. Blend until smooth. Add more frozen fruit and so on if desired. Smoothies should keep 3-plus days in the fridge and up to 3 months in the freezer. Freeze in covered serving-size containers for convenience.

*To freeze bananas, peel ripe bananas, break in 3 pieces, and place in 2 flat layers in sandwich bags. Seal bags and freeze.

Fruit Smoothie

Yield: 2 servings

1 cup apple or pineapple juice

1 apple, quartered

1 orange, peeled

1 large banana, cut in pieces

ice, optional

Put juice and fruit in blender and blend. If using frozen bananas, add slowly and blend until smooth. Add ice to thicken if desired.

Variation: Apples and oranges may be replaced with any seasonal or frozen fruit such as strawberries, apricots, peaches, pears, and so on.

Green Power Smoothie

Yield: 4-6 servings

An energizing drink that is good any time of day. Ingredients and amounts used are your choice and each drink you make will be different. You choose!

1–2 large handfuls fresh greens, chopped: kale, spinach, spring mix, beet greens, swiss chard, celery, cabbage, romaine, carrots, etc.

2 cups water or apple juice, plus more if desired

1–2 Tbsp. lemon juice or apple cider vinegar

2 Tbsp. flaxseed or meal

1 handful raw almonds

¼–½ tsp. cayenne pepper, optional

1 medium beet, peeled and cut

1 apple or pear, chopped

1 cup frozen berry mix

1–2 bananas, cut

1 piece ginger root, peeled

½–1 cup oats

1 Tbsp. powdered greens, optional

1–2 Tbsp. honey or agave, or to taste

Wash greens. In blender, put water or apple juice, lemon juice or vinegar, flaxseed or meal, almonds, cayenne if desired, beet, and fresh greens. Blend. Add apple or pear, frozen berry mix, and bananas and blend. Add ginger root, oats, and powdered greens (if desired) and blend until smooth. Add water or juice to thin if desired. Blend until very smooth, adding honey or agave to taste. Refrigerate or freeze. Freeze in covered serving-size containers for convenience.

Warm Breakfast Smoothie

Yield: 1 large serving

Very satisfying. Ideal for children whose braces have just been tightened!

½ cup water
⅓ cup oats
⅛ tsp. salt

1 banana
⅓ cup applesauce
½ cup yogurt, any flavor

Microwave water, oats, and salt for 1 minute on high. Put hot oatmeal into blender. Add banana, applesauce, and yogurt. Blend on high until smooth. Sip as you go and you'll be energized all morning!

Breakfast Smoothie

Yield: 3 to 4 servings

A quick and tasty breakfast.

2 cups apple juice, water, or milk
2 Tbsp. flaxseed meal
1 scoop protein powder, optional
½–1 cup oats
2–3 kale leaves or handful spinach

1 apple, quartered
1 orange, peeled and quartered
1 carrot, peeled and cut in pieces
1 banana, broken in pieces
1 cup fresh or frozen fruit, any kind

Place liquid, flaxseed meal, protein powder, oats, kale, apple, and orange in blender. Blend until smooth. Add carrot, banana, and fresh or frozen fruit. Blend until smooth. Add water for desired thickness. Smoothie freezes well in covered serving-size containers.

Strawberry-Banana Smoothie

Yield: 2 to 3 servings

This mixture can be frozen as fruit pops.

1 cup apple juice, orange juice, water, or milk

1 cup strawberries, fresh or frozen

1 banana, frozen in pieces

1 cup strawberry yogurt

ice (optional)

Combine liquid, strawberries, banana, and yogurt in blender. Blend until smooth. Slowly add ice cubes to thicken if desired. Serve immediately or refrigerate.

Fluffy Steamed Rice

Yield: 3 cups

An automatic rice cooker or a pressure cooker are time savers.

White Rice:

1 cup white rice

2 cups water

½ tsp. salt

Brown Rice:

1 cup brown rice

2½ cups water

½ tsp. salt

Combine rice, water, and salt in 2-quart pan. Bring to a boil, reduce heat, cover tightly, and let simmer. For white rice, simmer for 15 minutes, remove from heat, and let steam for 5–10 minutes. For brown rice, simmer for 40 minutes, remove from heat, and let steam for 5–10 minutes.

Rice 'n' Apple Breakfast

Yield: 4 to 6 servings

"Mmmm good" is the best way to describe this dish

½–1 cup apple juice or water
2–3 cups cooked rice
1 apple, diced

2–3 Tbsp. honey
¼ cup raisins
½ tsp. cinnamon

Combine all ingredients in a medium saucepan. Cover and simmer for 8–10 minutes over low heat, stirring occasionally. Or microwave on high for 4–6 minutes.

Rice 'n' Raisins

Yield: 4 servings

A quick breakfast.

1 cup white rice
2½ cups milk, or ⅔ cup dry milk
    and 2½ cups water

pinch of salt
¼ cup raisins
½ tsp. cinnamon

If using dry milk, mix with rice before adding water. Mix rice, milk or water, and salt in medium saucepan. Bring to boil, reduce heat, cover, and simmer for about 20 minutes or until rice is tender. Stir in raisins and cinnamon just before serving.

Oatmeal Plus

Yield: 3 to 4 servings

A large bowl of oatmeal in the morning helps keep you satisfied 'til lunch.

1 cup old-fashioned oats	**2–3 Tbsp. raisins**
½ tsp. salt	**2–3 Tbsp. sunflower seeds or chopped**
2 cups water	**almonds, optional**

Stir oats into boiling salted water. Add raisins and sunflower seeds. Simmer for 5–7 minutes. Cover and let stand for about 5 minutes.

Tip: You can also cook this in the microwave (2 minutes). Additionally, add ⅓ cup dried fruit—such as apples, berries, peaches, bananas, etc.—in place of raisins and sunflower seeds or almonds.

Cracked Wheat Cereal

Yield: 4 (½-cup) servings

Sticks to your ribs and helps you stay "regular."

½ cup whole wheat kernels	**2 cups water**
½ tsp. salt	

Place whole wheat in blender. Pulse or run on high speed for 20–30 seconds, until wheat is of desired consistency. Using whisk, gradually stir cracked wheat into salted water in a medium saucepan. Bring to a boil, stirring constantly. Reduce heat to low, cover, and let simmer until done, stirring occasionally. Cook for 12–15 minutes.

Microwave Cracked Wheat Cereal

Yield: 1 serving

This recipe is an easy way to fix one serving.

1 cup water   **pinch of salt**

**⅓ cup cracked wheat or 9-grain
   cereal**

Mix ingredients in microwave-safe container. Cover and micro-wave for 3–4 minutes and then stir. If cereal is too thin, cook a little longer or let stand a few minutes. The grain absorbs moisture as it stands.

Whole Wheat Cereal

Yield: 2 cups cooked wheat Wheat doubles in size when cooked. It makes a nour-ishing breakfast and is a good addition to soups, salads ,or casseroles. Cooked wheat stores well in the refrigerator.

**1 cup whole-kernel wheat
   berries**   **½ tsp. salt**

2 cups water

Place wheat, water, and salt in medium saucepan. Bring to a boil and then reduce heat to simmer. Cover and cook for 45–60 minutes or until wheat is tender and chewy.

Tip: You can also make this in a slow cooker (overnight or 8 hours on low).

Thermos: Place wheat, boiling water, and salt in a widemouthed 1–2 quart ther-mos. Cover tightly. Let sit overnight or about 8 hours. The wheat will swell into plump, chewy kernels. Reheat just before serving if desired. Enjoy as cereal or use in soup, stews, or casseroles. Store covered in refrigerator.

Millet Cereal

Yield: 6 servings

Millet makes for a healthy breakfast.

2 cups water
½ tsp. salt
½ cup millet

1 apple, chopped, optional
¼ cup raisins, optional
cinnamon and sugar, optional

Bring water and salt to a boil. Add millet. Reduce heat to low, cover, and steam for 25–30 minutes. Don't stir. Optional: add apple to top of millet the last 5 minutes; serve with raisins and a light sprinkle of cinnamon and sugar.

Cornmeal Mush

Yield: 6 servings

Pioneers often ate this nutritious mush.

1 cup cornmeal
1 cup cold water

3 cups boiling water
½ tsp. salt

In a large, heavy saucepan, mix cornmeal and cold water until smooth. Use a whisk and stir boiling water and salt into cornmeal mixture. Cook, stirring constantly, until mixture thickens and boils. Reduce heat, cover, and cook for 10 minutes.

Fried Cornmeal Mush

Grandpa enjoyed eating this fried mush.

Pour leftover Cornmeal Mush (p. XX) into greased loaf pan and chill until firm. Slice and fry mush slowly in hot oil in skillet, turning once. Serve with butter, maple syrup, or jelly. This fried mush complements most any meal.

Granola Plus

Yield: 14 to 16 cups

Granola makes a great breakfast or a delicious high-energy snack. Vary these tasty recipes with ingredients that are available.

8–10 cups oats	1½ cups brown sugar or honey
1 cup sunflower seeds	1 tsp. salt
1–2 cups sliced or coarsely chopped almonds	2 tsp. maple flavoring or vanilla
1 cup whole wheat flour	1 cup coconut
1 cup bran, optional	1–2 cups raisins and/or dried cranberries
1 cup water	½ cup dried fruit: pineapple, apples, bananas, etc.
½ cup oil	

Preheat oven to 325°F. In large bowl, mix oats, sunflower seeds, almonds, flour, and bran (if desired). Whisk together (or use blender to thoroughly mix) water, oil, brown sugar or honey, salt, and maple flavoring or vanilla. Pour over dry ingredients, stirring to coat well. Spread on 2 large greased baking sheets. Bake until golden, 30–40 minutes. Remove from oven. Add coconut, raisins and/or dried cranberries, and dried fruit of choice. Store covered in cool place. Granola keeps well.

Tip: For crispy granola, Turn off oven when done, but leave granola in oven until cool.

Granola

Yield: about 8 cups

Ideal for a small batch.

5 cups oats

1 cup sunflower seeds

1 cup sliced or chopped almonds

3 Tbsp. ground flaxseed

½ cup brown sugar

½ tsp. salt

⅓ cup water

¼ cup oil

½ cup honey or pure maple syrup

1 tsp. vanilla

2 cups dried fruit: raisins, pineapple, etc.

Preheat oven to 300°F. Combine oats, sunflower seeds, almonds, ground flaxseed, brown sugar, and salt in large bowl. Mix water, oil, honey or maple syrup, and vanilla. Pour mixture over dry ingredients and mix thoroughly. Spread on large greased baking sheet. Bake for 35–45 minutes or until golden, stirring twice during baking. Granola becomes crunchy as it cools. Add dried fruit and store covered in a cool place.

Omelets For a Crowd

Everyone makes their own personalized omelet. Use quart-size bags and write a name on each bag with a permanent marker.

2 eggs per bag

quart-size freezer bags

2 Tbsp. water per bag

fillings (p. XX)

salsa, optional

Crack 2 eggs into each quart-size freezer bag. Add water. Seal and shake well. Add fillings as desired. Remove all air from bags and seal. Shake well to mix ingredients. Place 6–8 bags into a large pot of rolling, boiling water for 13 minutes. Cut the bag, and the omelet will roll out easily. Serve with salsa if desired.

Omelet Deluxe

Yield: 1 large omelet

2 eggs
2 Tbsp. water
⅛ tsp. salt

1 Tbsp. butter
favorite fillings (see below)
salsa, optional

Beat eggs, water, and salt with fork, wire whisk, or blender. Heat 10-inch skillet until hot enough to sizzle a few drops of water. Add butter to skillet. Pour in egg mixture and cook quickly, pushing cooked edges toward center and tilting pan to allow uncooked egg to flow to edges. Slide pan rapidly back and forth over heat to keep mixture in motion and moving freely. While eggs are still moist and shiny on top, place desired fillings (see below) on one side of the omelet. With pancake turner, fold omelet in half, let sit a few seconds, and turn out onto plate with a quick flip of the wrist. Top with salsa if desired. Makes 1 delicious serving.

Precooked Filling Suggestions:

- Diced potatoes
- Diced ham or turkey
- Bacon or sausage
- Peas and carrots
- Asparagus
- Chopped broccoli

Other Filling Suggestions:

- Diced tomatoes
- Diced green or red peppers
- Chopped green onions
- Shredded cheese
- Cottage cheese
- Mushrooms

Breakfast Casserole

Yield: 12 servings

Prepare this savory dish the day before and bake just before serving.

¼ cup diced green pepper

6 green onions, diced

2 slices bread

1 cup diced ham or cooked
   sausage

2 potatoes, cooked and diced

6 eggs

2 cups milk, or 2 cups water and
   ½ cup dry milk

½ tsp. salt

1 tsp. dry mustard

1 (4-oz.) can mushrooms,
   drained

⅓ cup parmesan cheese

Microwave green pepper and onions in 1 tablespoon water until tender. While vegetables are cooking, cube bread and spread in the bottom of a greased 9×13 baking dish. Spread ham or sausage and potatoes evenly over bread. Combine eggs, milk (or water and dry milk), salt, and dry mustard in blender. Blend until mixed. Pour mixture over bread, ham, and potatoes. Top with green pepper, onions, and mushrooms. Sprinkle with parmesan cheese. Cover and refrigerate overnight if desired. Preheat oven to 350°F. Bake uncovered for 30–40 minutes.

Breakfast Wrap

Yield: 1 to 2 servings

Enjoy a quick nourishing breakfast on the run.

2 eggs, beaten

2 Tbsp. salsa

dash of salt

shredded cheese, optional

flour tortilla or whole wheat
   toast

Mix eggs, salsa, and salt. Cook in oiled skillet until eggs are set but still shiny. Serve wrapped in warm tortilla or on whole wheat toast.

Hash Browns

Yield: 4 to 6 servings

Fresh potato hash browns have a crunchy outside, moist and tender inside.

2 Tbsp. oil
4 raw potatoes, shredded

salt and pepper to taste
2 Tbsp. water

Heat oil in a large skillet. Add shredded potatoes and season to taste with salt and pepper. Turn heat to low and cover pan. Do not stir. Cook for 5–8 minutes. Using a large spatula, turn all the potatoes at once. Add water, season again, and replace lid. Continue cooking another 5–8 minutes or until potatoes are crunchy and golden on the outside, tender on the inside.

Cooked Potato Hash Browns

Yield: 4 to 6 servings

2 Tbsp. oil
4 cooked potatoes, shredded or
   diced

salt and pepper to taste

Heat 2 tablespoons oil in large skillet and add potatoes. Season to taste with salt and pepper. Fry about 3 minutes on each side, turning with a pancake turner. Serve hot.

French Toast

Yield: 4 slices

A flavorful way to use day-old bread.

1 egg, beaten
½ cup milk

pinch of salt
4 slices bread

Mix egg, milk ,and salt with a whisk until frothy. Pour egg mixture into pie tin or other shallow pan. Quickly dip bread slices, one at a time, into the egg mixture. Cook on 350-degree nonstick griddle until golden brown.

Favorite Pancakes or Waffles

Yield: about 12 (2-inch) pancakes

An easy-to-remember and easy-to-double recipe with two mixing options. Make light or extra-light pancakes!

1 cup whole wheat or white flour

1 Tbsp. sugar or honey

1 Tbsp. baking powder

¼ tsp. salt

1 egg

1 cup milk, or ¼ cup dry milk and 1 scant cup water

1 Tbsp. oil

Combine flour, sugar or honey, baking powder, and salt. If using dry milk, add to dry ingredients. Beat egg until light and fluffy—this is the secret of light pancakes. Whisk in egg, milk or water, and oil, mixing just until dry ingredients are well moistened. Batter will be slightly lumpy. Add more milk if thin pancakes are desired or a little more flour if you prefer them thick. Cook on 350-degree griddle, turning once, or bake in hot waffle iron.

Apple Pancakes: Fold in ½ cup grated apple just before cooking.

Blueberry Pancakes: Fold in 1 cup blueberries just before cooking.

Banana Pancakes: Add thin slices of banana to each pancake as they cook.

Extra-Light Pancakes or Waffles: Mix flour, sugar or honey, baking powder, and salt in bowl. Separate egg. Add milk, oil, and egg yolk to dry ingredients and whisk together thoroughly. Beat egg white until stiff and gently fold into the batter. Cook immediately on hot griddle or in waffle iron.

Blender Pancakes or Waffles

Yield: 12 to 14 pancakes

This tasty recipe has helped many families transition into using whole wheat. A great recipe for cooks without a wheat grinder!

1¼ cups milk, or water and
¼ cup dry milk

1 cup wheat kernels

2 Tbsp. oil

1 large egg

2 Tbsp. honey or sugar

½ tsp. salt

1 Tbsp. baking powder

Put milk (or water and dry milk) and wheat kernels in blender. Blend on high for 3–4 minutes, until mixture is smooth. (A heavy duty blender may only take about 1 minute.) Add oil, egg, honey or sugar, and salt. Blend until smooth. Add baking powder and pulse about 3 times or blend just enough to mix well. Mixture will foam up and get very light. Cook immediately on hot nonstick griddle or in waffle iron.

Oatmeal Pancakes or Waffles

Yield: 12 to 15 large pancakes or about 36 (2-inch) pancakes

A hearty stick-to-your-ribs meal.

1 cup whole wheat or white
flour

1 cup oats

1 Tbsp. brown sugar

1 Tbsp. baking powder

1 tsp. salt

2 eggs, well beaten

2 Tbsp. oil

1½ cups milk, or 1½ cups water
and ⅓ cup dry milk

Combine flour, oats, brown sugar, baking powder, and salt. If using dry milk, mix into dry ingredients. Whisk in eggs, oil, and milk or water and mix just until dry ingredients are well moistened. Let sit a few minutes to soften oats. Thin with water if needed. Spread about ⅓ cup batter on hot griddle to make large pancakes.

GF Pancakes: Follow above recipe using 2 cups oat flour (blend oats to equal 2 cups flour). Add 1 tablespoon cornstarch. These pancakes may also be used for bread.

Pancake Master Mix

Yield: enough mix for 275 (3-inch) pancakes

Nutritious whole grain pancakes are quick and easy to make using this mix.

10 cups whole wheat flour	**4 tsp. salt**
2 cups white flour	**2/3 cup sugar**
2/3 cup baking powder	**2 cups dry milk**

Combine flour, baking powder, salt, sugar, and dry milk and mix well. Store mix in a covered container in a cool, dry place. Use as directed in recipe below.

Tip: All whole wheat flour, all white flour, or half and half can be used.

Pancakes (using Master Mix)

Yield: 8 to 10 (3-inch) pancakes

1 egg, beaten	**1 Tbsp. oil**
¾ cup water	**1 cup Pancake Master Mix (recipe above)**

In medium bowl, beat egg until light. Stir in water and oil. Add Pancake Master Mix and stir just until ingredients are combined. Add additional pancake mix or water if needed for desired consistency. Cook on 350- to 375-degree nonstick griddle.

Maple or Cinnamon Syrup

Yield: about 2½ cups

Make your own syrup and save money.

1 cup sugar or honey

1 Tbsp. cornstarch

1½–2 cups water or juice

1 tsp. maple flavoring;
or 1 tsp. vanilla, 1 tsp.
cinnamon, 1 tsp. allspice

Mix sugar and cornstarch in a small saucepan. Add water or juice and whisk until smooth. If using honey, mix cornstarch in a small amount of the water before adding honey and remaining water. Cook and stir over medium heat until mixture comes to a boil and is slightly thickened. Stir in maple flavoring or vanilla, cinnamon, and allspice.

Fruit Syrup: Follow recipe above. Use grape, plum, berry, apple, or chokecherry juice in place of water. Omit flavoring and spices.

Fruit Topping

Yield: 2 cups

Delicious served on pancakes, cheesecake, and so on.

1½ cups fruit; fresh or frozen,
whole or pureed (blueberries,
peaches strawberries, etc.)

⅓ cup sugar or honey

1 Tbsp. cornstarch

½ cup apple juice

In saucepan, mix fruit, sugar or honey, cornstarch, and apple juice. Bring to a boil over medium heat, stirring constantly, and cook just until thick, 3–5 minutes.

Honey Butter

Yield: 1½ cups

Making good fluffy honey butter is almost a lost art.

1 cube butter, softened　　　　　**1 tsp. vanilla**
½ cup honey

Whip butter until light and fluffy. Slowly add honey and vanilla. Adding honey too rapidly makes butter lose its thick, fluffy consistency. Whip 2–3 more minutes. Cover and refrigerate. Serve at room temperature. Stores well.

Raspberry Butter: Add ⅓ cup raspberry jam to Honey Butter and whip 2–3 more minutes.

Yogurt

Making yogurt is easy and economical. This recipe and the next are excellent.

½ cup dry milk　　　　　　　**1 pkg. freeze-dried yogurt**
1 quart milk　　　　　　　　　　**starter or ½ cup plain**
　　　　　　　　　　　　　　　　　unflavored yogurt with
　　　　　　　　　　　　　　　　　active culture

Combine dry milk and milk using blender or wire whisk. In saucepan, slowly heat milk to scalding temperature, 180°F, stirring often. Maintain this temperature for 2 minutes. This makes a superior-quality yogurt and is worth the few minutes it takes. Remove milk from heat and cool to lukewarm, 115°F. Stir yogurt starter or plain yogurt into 1 cup of the milk. Pour the mixture back into the rest of the milk and whisk together to mix well. Then follow directions in numbers 2, 3, and 4 on next page.

Yogurt from Dry Milk

Yield: 4 cups

2 cups non-instant dry milk or 3 cups instant dry milk

4 cups warm water (125°F)

1 package yogurt starter or ½ cup plain yogurt with active culture

1. **Using wire whisk,** combine dry milk with warm water. When milk mixes in and is dissolved, stir in yogurt starter or yogurt.

2. **Incubate mixture** undisturbed for 8–12 hours or until yogurt reaches desired consistency. This can be done in an electric yogurt maker, a widemouth vacuum bottle, or a widemouth jar wrapped in several layers of towel or blanket (wool is best).

   Or place mixture in quart jar in a pan of warm water over an electric burner turned to warm (don't overheat) for 4–5 hours. Turn off heat and let stand until yogurt is firm. Chill before using. Yogurt stays fresh for several weeks in the refrigerator.

3. **Save ⅓ cup of the yogurt** for a starter. To make consistent, high-quality, mild-flavored yogurt, use a new yogurt starter every 3–4 batches.

4. **Serve with fresh fruit** or use in recipes that call for yogurt. Yogurt is a good alternative to sour cream or mayonnaise and a good source of calcium and protein.

CHAPTER 5

Savory Soups and Stews

During difficult times, bread and soup have been the primary foods consumed by people in most every culture. Bread in particular has a long history of being a diet staple during hardships. Our bread section in chapter 2 includes a large variety of both quick breads and yeast breads. However, you wouldn't have a balanced diet if all you had to eat was bread. But you could live on bread, particularly whole grain bread, and hearty nutritious soups—this combination can be both satisfying and life-sustaining.

Soups are delicious, are economical, and can be made with almost anything you have on hand. They can easily be increased by adding additional liquid. Soups are a great way to use freeze-dried or dehydrated vegetables. For amounts, simply follow instructions on the container. Soups are simple to cook as one-pot meals and don't require much in the way of fuel. They are easy to serve, requiring only a bowl or cup and a spoon, so they result in only minimal cleanup, which is always a plus.

Many hearty, delicious soup and stew recipes are included in this chapter. If you store basic ingredients needed to make nutritious soups and whole grain breads, you will be well on your way to enjoying a wide variety of balanced, nourishing meals now as well as in the tough times ahead. Good canned, freeze-dried, or dehydrated soups are also available and will add variety to your food storage and your diet.

Chicken Noodle Soup

Yield: 4 to 5 servings

6 cups water

3 Tbsp. chicken bouillon or 3 (15-oz.) cans chicken broth

1 onion, minced, or 2 Tbsp. dry chopped onion

1 tsp. minced garlic

3 carrots, peeled and sliced

2 stalks celery, sliced

½ tsp. salt

1 cup thick dry noodles

1 (10-oz.) can cream of chicken soup

1 cup canned diced chicken, with liquid

Place water and bouillon or broth in large soup pot. Add onion, garlic, carrots, celery and salt. Bring to a boil. Add noodles and simmer until noodles are tender, about 12 minutes. Stir in soup and chicken. Bring to a boil. Serve hot.

Chicken and Wild Rice Soup

Yield: 6 to 8 servings

A satisfying soup to make for family or a sick friend.

8 cups water

1 (4- to 6-oz.) box long grain and wild rice plus seasoning mix, or ½ cup long grain rice plus 1 Tbsp. chicken bouillon

1 pkg. dry chicken noodle soup mix or ¼ cup broken spaghetti noodles

1 medium onion, diced, or 2 Tbsp. dry chopped onion

3–4 carrots, thinly sliced, or 1 (14-oz.) can carrots, with liquid

2–3 stalks celery, thinly sliced

1–2 cups finely shredded cabbage, optional

1 (10-oz.) can cream of chicken soup

1 large chicken breast, cooked and diced, or 1–2 cups canned diced chicken, with liquid

In large soup pot, put 8 cups water, rice plus seasoning mix, chicken noodle soup mix, onion, carrots, celery, and cabbage. Bring to a boil, reduce heat, and simmer for 15–20 minutes. When vegetables are tender, add cream of chicken soup and stir gently until blended. Thin with additional water if desired. Stir in chicken. Heat and serve.

Chicken Vegetable Soup

Yield: 12 to 15 servings

A hearty, delicious, and nutritious soup that feeds a crowd. Use freeze-dried or dehydrated vegetables if desired.

1 leftover rotisserie chicken or turkey carcass

12–14 cups water

1 large onion, chopped, or 2 Tbsp. dry chopped onion

1–2 tsp. salt

2 (14-oz.) cans diced or stewed tomatoes

6–8 cups fresh or frozen chopped vegetables (celery, carrots, potatoes, broccoli, mushrooms, etc.)

1–2 tsp. basil

1 Tbsp. chicken bouillon

1 cup broken spaghetti or noodles, uncooked

Place chicken or turkey carcass in large pan. Add water, onion, and salt. Bring to a boil and simmer about 20 minutes. Cool slightly. Remove carcass from pan. Debone meat and set aside. Strain broth if desired. Add tomatoes, chopped vegetables, basil, and chicken bouillon. Cover, bring to a boil, and simmer for 20–35 minutes. Add uncooked pasta and deboned meat. Add more water if needed. Simmer for 12–15 minutes or until noodles are tender.

Minestrone Soup

Yield: 6 to 8 servings

This soup tastes even better the second day.

1 (14-oz.) can pork and beans

1 (10-oz.) can minestrone soup or vegetable beef soup

1 soup can full of water

1 onion, chopped, or 2 Tbsp. dry chopped onion

¼ cup barbecue sauce

1 (14-oz.) can diced tomatoes

1 tsp. basil

Optional, but recommended:

1 potato, chopped

2 stalks celery, chopped

2 carrots, chopped

In large, heavy saucepan, mix pork and beans, minestrone soup, water, onion, barbecue sauce, tomatoes, and basil. Microwave potato, celery, and carrots for about 6 minutes and then add to soup mixture if desired. The vegetables are a very tasty addition. Simmer soup for 10– 20 minutes.

Potato Soup

Yield: 6 to 8 servings

A delicious creamy soup

2 cups water

1 large onion, chopped, or 2–3 Tbsp. dry chopped onion

2 stalks celery

1 tsp. salt

5–6 large potatoes, peeled and diced

3–4 cups milk, or 3–4 cups water and 1 cup dry milk

1 (10-oz.) can cream of celery soup, optional

In large saucepan, mix water, onion, celery, salt, and diced potatoes. Cook until potatoes are mushy and tender. Stir in milk or water and celery soup (if desired). If using dry milk, whisk or blend into water before adding to soup. Remove 2 cups of the potato mixture, puree in blender, and stir back into soup. Heat through and serve.

Tortellini Soup

Yield: 8 servings

A quick and tasty meal.

1–2 Tbsp. minced garlic

1 small onion, minced

1 medium carrot, chopped

2 Tbsp. oil

3 (14-oz.) chicken broth

1 (14-oz). can diced tomatoes

4 cups water

1 tsp. basil

dash of pepper; salt to taste

1 (9-oz.) pkg. dried, cheese-filled tortellini, or 2–3 cups wide noodles

1 (14-oz.) can cooked white beans, with liquid (2 cups)

4 cups fresh baby spinach, coarsely chopped, or 1 (14-oz.) can chopped spinach

In 6-quart pan, sauté garlic, onion, and carrot in oil over medium heat for 3–5 minutes. Stir in chicken broth, tomatoes, water, basil, and pepper and salt. Bring to a boil and reduce heat. Stir in tortellini and beans. Cover and simmer for about 20 minutes, stirring occasionally. Don't boil or tortellini may burst. Add spinach. Cover and simmer for 8–10 minutes but don't overcook.

Winter Soup

Yield: 6 to 8 servings

Good soup couldn't be easier.

1 (14-oz.) can green beans, with liquid

1 (14-oz.) can whole kernel corn, with liquid

2 (14-oz.) cans stewed tomatoes

2 tsp. chili powder, or to taste

salt and pepper to taste

1 cup cooked ground beef, optional

Mix green beans, corn, and tomatoes in a large saucepan. Add chili powder plus salt and pepper to taste. Add ground beef if desired. Simmer until soup is hot and bubbly, about 10 minutes.

Cabin Stew

Yield: 4 to 5 servings

Makes a hearty meal in a hurry.

1 (24-oz.) can beef stew
1 (14-oz). can chili with beans

1 (10-oz.) can vegetable soup

Mix all ingredients in saucepan. Heat to boiling and simmer for 10 minutes. Thin with a little water if desired.

Vegetable Beef Stew

Yield: 6 servings

Serve hot biscuits with this nourishing meal.

1 lb. lean stew meat, trimmed and cut
2 (14-oz.) cans stewed or diced tomatoes
2 cups water
6 carrots, peeled and cubed
4 celery stalks, cut in 1-inch pieces

6 large potatoes, peeled and cut
2 large onions, diced, or ¼ cup dry chopped onion
¼ cup raw pearled barley
1 tsp. salt
¼ tsp. pepper
6 cups hot steamed brown rice (2 cups raw)

Brown meat in a little oil in a large saucepan. Add tomatoes, water, carrots, celery, potatoes, onions, barley, salt, and pepper. Simmer for 2–3 hours or cook in oven all day at 250°F. Serve over steamed rice.

Tip: This stew may also be prepared in a slow cooker. Cook on low for 6–8 hours or on high for 3–4 hours.

Beef Stew

Yield: 6 to 8 servings

This hearty stew is delicious and quick using a pressure cooker.

¼ cup flour

1–2 tsp. salt; dash of pepper

1 lb. lean beef stew meat, cubed

2 Tbsp. oil

2 Tbsp. cider vinegar

1 large onion, diced, or 2 Tbsp. dry chopped onion

4–6 cups water

3 beef bouillon cubes

3 Tbsp. catsup

1 tsp. basil

1 Tbsp. Worcestershire sauce

4 large carrots, cut in 1-inch pieces

2 stalks celery, cut in 1-inch pieces

4–5 potatoes, cut in 1-inch cubes

Combine flour and salt and pepper in a paper or plastic bag. Add meat and shake until well coated with flour mixture. Heat oil in a large saucepan, add beef, and cook until brown on all sides. Stir in vinegar, onion, water, bouillon, catsup, basil, and Worcestershire sauce. Pressure cook or slow cook if desired. Or simmer for 30–45 minutes. Add carrots, celery, and potatoes. Stir and heat until mixture boils. Lower heat and simmer until vegetables are just tender.

Tip: For pressure cooker, follow directions on cooker. For slow cooker, cook on low for 4–5 hours.

Stew in Five Minutes

Yield: about 8 servings

Fix this tasty no-fuss soup in minutes.

1 (10-oz.) can tomato soup, undiluted

1 (10-oz.) can vegetable beef soup, undiluted

1 (14-oz.) can chili con carne, with beans

1 (14-oz.) can whole kernel corn, with liquid

1 (14-oz.) can green beans, with liquid

1 cup water

In large saucepan mix all ingredients. Heat to boiling, simmer, and serve.

Hamburger Soup

Yield: 10 to 12 servings

A favorite recipe using basics.

½–1 lb. lean ground beef

1 large onion, chopped, or 2 Tbsp. dry chopped onion

3 stalks celery, diced

4 potatoes, cubed

3 carrots, diced

2 cups chopped cabbage

2 (14-oz.) cans tomatoes

1 can corn, with liquid

1 cup rice, noodles, or macaroni

4–6 cups water

2–3 tsp. salt

¼ tsp. pepper

1 Tsp. Worcestershire or soy sauce

In large saucepan, brown ground beef and onion. Drain well. Add celery, potatoes, carrots, cabbage, tomatoes, corn, rice or noodles, water, salt, pepper, and Worcestershire or soy sauce. Soup should not be too thick, so add more water if needed. Bring to a boil and then lower heat, cover, and simmer for 30–40 minutes until vegetables are tender and flavors blend.

Tip: To cook with a slow cooker, turn to low for 4–6 hours

Squash Soup

Yield: 8 to 10 Servings

Nutritious and satisfying.

1 medium butternut squash, peeled and cubed

2 yams, peeled and cubed

3 carrots, peeled and cut into thick slices

1 large onion, peeled and quartered

1 (32-oz.) can chicken broth (4 cups)

salt and pepper to taste

Cook squash, yams, carrots, and onion in broth in saucepan until tender, 25–30 minutes. Cool slightly. Blend until smooth. Season to taste.

Creamy Taco Soup

Yield: 6 to 8 servings

Simply the best taco soup we've eaten.

1 (14-oz.) can refried beans

1 (14-oz.) can Mexican stewed tomatoes, with liquid

1 (14-oz.) can diced tomatoes, with liquid

1 (14-oz.) can black beans, with liquid

1 (14-oz.) can kidney beans, with liquid

1 (14-oz.) can whole kernel corn, with liquid

1 onion, chopped, or 1–2 Tbsp. dry chopped onion

1–2 Tbsp. chili powder or taco seasoning, to taste

In large saucepan, mix refried beans, stewed tomatoes (blended slightly if desired), diced tomatoes, black beans, kidney beans, corn, onion, and chili powder. Stir and cook over medium heat until mixture comes to a boil. Let simmer for 10–15 minutes. Thin with a little water if needed. Serve with corn chips, cheese, sour cream, or cornbread if desired.

Taco Soup

Yield: 8 to 10 servings

A hearty soup full of rich flavor.

1 lb. lean ground beef

1 large onion, chopped, or 2 Tbsp. dry chopped onion

1 (46-oz.) can tomato juice or mixed vegetable juice

1 (8-oz.) can tomato sauce

1 (14-oz.) can red kidney beans, with liquid

1 (14-oz.) can black beans, with liquid

1 (14-oz.) can whole kernel corn, with liquid

2–3 Tbsp. taco seasoning or chili powder, to taste

In large pan, brown ground beef and onion. Drain fat and discard. Add tomato juice, tomato sauce, beans, corn, and taco seasoning. Thin with a little water if desired. Simmer for 20–30 minutes.

White Chili

Yield: 6 servings

A good way to enjoy canned chicken or turkey.

1 (14-oz.) can tomatoes

2 (14-oz.) cans white or pinto beans, with liquid

1–2 cups diced cooked chicken or turkey, with liquid

2 Tbsp. dry chopped onion

2 tsp. chili powder

2 cups water

1 tsp. sugar

salt to taste

In large pan over medium-high heat, mix tomatoes, beans with liquid, chicken or turkey, onion, chili powder, water, sugar, and salt. Heat to boiling and simmer for about 10 minutes to blend flavors, stirring occasionally.

Nine-Bean Mix

Use equal parts

pearled barley

red beans

pinto beans

navy beans

Great Northern beans

lentils

split peas

black beans

black-eyed peas

Nine-Bean Soup

Yield: 8 servings

Enjoy the unique blend of flavors. A nine-bean mix is available at most markets or see above.

1 large onion, chopped, or
  2 Tbsp. dry chopped onion

1 Tbsp. minced garlic

8 cups water

2 cups dry 9-bean mix (above)

1 lean ham hock or ham bone,
  or 1 (5-oz.) can diced ham

1 (4-oz.) can diced green chilies

1 (14-oz.) can diced tomatoes

3 Tbsp. fresh lemon juice

salt to taste

Chop onion and garlic in blender, using a small amount of the water. Put beans, water, ham hock, onion and garlic in slow cooker and cook for 3 hours on high or all day on low, or until beans are just tender. Soaking beans overnight reduces cooking time. (Instead of a slow cooker, you can simmer in a large pan on the stove for 3–4 hours.) Add remaining ingredients and cook 1 more hour. This soup is easy to make and is even more delicious the second day.

Black Bean Soup

Yield: 6 servings

Quick, tasty, and satisfying. Easy to double and feed a crowd

2 (14-oz.) cans black beans, with liquid

2 cups salsa, mild or medium

1 cup water

2 tsp. beef or chicken bouillon

1 tsp. sugar

3 cups cooked rice

In heavy saucepan, stir together beans, salsa, water, and bouillon. Simmer for 15–20 minutes. Serve in bowls over hot cooked rice.

Ham and White Bean Soup

Yield: about 10 to 12 servings

This flavorful soup always brings compliments.

1 onion, diced, or 2 Tbsp. dry chopped onion

1 Tbsp. minced garlic

10 cups water

2 cups white beans

1 lean, meaty ham bone, or ham hock, or 1 cup diced ham, or 1 (5-oz.) can ham, diced, with liquid

2 potatoes, peeled and cubed

2 stalks celery, thinly sliced

2–3 carrots, peeled and diced

2–3 tsp. salt

1 tsp. liquid smoke, optional

In blender, chop onion and garlic in 1 cup of the water if desired. Place beans and water in large saucepan. Add onion, garlic, and ham bone to beans. Cover saucepan and cook until beans are just tender, about 2 hours. Remove ham bone; cool slightly and remove meat from bone. Add ham, potatoes, celery, carrots, salt, and liquid smoke to saucepan. Cook 30–45 more minutes or until beans and vegetables are tender.

Split Pea Soup

Yield: 8 to 10 servings

A delicious and satisfying family favorite.

2 cups split peas

8–10 cups water

1 large onion, diced, or 2 Tbsp.
  dry chopped onion

2 medium potatoes, cubed

2–3 carrots, diced

3 celery stalks, diced

salt to taste

¼ tsp. pepper

¼ tsp. marjoram

¼ tsp. thyme leaves

½ tsp. liquid smoke

1 cup diced ham, or 1 (5-oz.)
  can ham, diced

1–2 Tbsp. instant mashed
  potatoes, optional

Place peas, water, onion, potatoes, carrots, celery, salt, pepper, marjoram, thyme, and liquid smoke in a large heavy saucepan. Bring to a boil. Cover and reduce heat to low. Simmer for 1–2 hours or until peas are tender. Use a stick blender or blender to puree soup. Thin with water or chicken broth if desired. For a thicker soup, stir in instant mashed potatoes. Add diced ham. Heat and serve. Soup freezes well.

Tip: You can cook this in a slow cooker on low for 4–6 hours.

Tip: No time to chop vegetables? Cook split peas in 6 cups of the water for about 45 minutes, stirring often. Use a blender to puree vegetables in the remaining 3-4 cups water. Add to peas, bring to a boil, and simmer over low heat for 45–60 minutes, stirring occasionally. Makes a smooth creamy soup with little preparation time.

Creamy Split Pea Soup

Yield: 6 to 8 servings

Smooth, flavorful, and easy to make,

2 cups dry split peas

8 cups water

1 onion, chopped, or 2 Tbsp.
   dry chopped onion

2 tsp. salt

¼ tsp. pepper

ham bone or bacon, optional

1 (12-oz.) can evaporated milk

Place split peas, water, onion, salt, and pepper in large saucepan. Add ham bone or bacon if desired. Bring mixture to a boil. Cover and simmer until peas are tender, 1–2 hours. Remove meat, if used. Stir in evaporated milk. Add ham or bacon if desired. Heat to a simmer but don't boil.

Quick Lentil Soup

Yield: 4 to 6 servings

This soup is delicious and couldn't be easier.

2 cups lentils, sorted and
   washed

8 cups water

1 carrot, finely chopped

1 onion, finely chopped, or 2
   Tbsp. dry chopped onion

1–2 chicken bouillon cubes

1 (24-oz.) jar pasta sauce of
   choice

1–2 tsp. sugar (to taste)

Place lentils and water in large heavy saucepan with carrot, onion, and bouillon. Bring to a boil. Reduce to simmer and cook until tender, 20–30 minutes. Stir in pasta sauce. Stir soup and simmer for another 5–8 minutes.

Tip: Blend carrot and onion in 1 cup of the water. Add to soup and cook.

Lentil Vegetable Soup

Yield: 6 servings

The perfect soup for a brisk fall day, and a favorite soup for children.

2 cups lentils, sorted and washed

6 cups water

1 Tbsp. minced garlic

1 medium onion, chopped, or 2 Tbsp. dry chopped onion

1 carrot, chopped

1 stalk celery, chopped

1 (14-oz.) can diced tomatoes

1–2 chicken bouillon cubes

1 Tbsp. dry parsley

1 tsp. salt

¼ tsp. pepper

¼ tsp. thyme

1 (10-oz.) pkg. frozen chopped spinach, or 1 (14-oz.) can spinach

Place lentils and water in large saucepan. Bring to a boil and simmer uncovered for 15 minutes. Add garlic, onion, carrot, and celery and simmer until tender, 5–7 minutes. Add tomatoes, bouillon, parsley, salt, pepper, and thyme. Heat to boiling. Reduce heat, cover, and simmer for 20–25 minutes. Add spinach during the last 15 minutes.

Tip: You can cook this in a slow cooker on low for 4–6 hours.

Chicken Barley Soup

Yield: 10 to 12 servings

A hearty, flavorful soup full of vegetables.

8 cups water

2 Tbsp. chicken bouillon

3–4 chicken thighs, or 2 cups canned cubed chicken, with liquid

1 cup pearled barley

1 large onion, diced, or 2 Tbsp. dry chopped onion

1 Tbsp. minced garlic

3 stalks celery, chopped

3 large carrots, sliced

1 cup chopped broccoli

1 (14-oz.) can crushed or diced tomatoes

1 (14-oz.) can black beans, with liquid

2 tsp. basil

1 Tbsp. parsley flakes

1 Tbsp. teriyaki or soy sauce

salt to taste

In large soup pot, add water, bouillon, chicken thighs, barley, onion, garlic, celery, carrots, broccoli, tomatoes, black beans with liquid, basil, parsley flakes, teriyaki or soy sauce, and salt to taste. Bring to a boil, lower heat, cover, and simmer until chicken and barley are tender, 40–50 minutes. Remove chicken thighs from soup and let cool slightly. Discard skin, remove chicken from bones, and cut into bite-size pieces. Return meat to soup, or add the canned chicken and broth. Thin soup with water if desired.

Tip: You can cook this in a slow cooker, on low for 4–6 hours, or in a pressure cooker for about 15 minutes.

Palestine Stew

Yield: 8 to 10 servings

To make this gluten-free, use quinoa or other gluten-free grain in place of wheat.

1 lb. ground beef

1 onion, chopped, or 2 Tbsp.
   dry chopped onion

1 cup whole wheat kernels

1 cup lentils

4 cups water

2 (14-oz.) cans crushed
   tomatoes

1 tsp. salt

½ tsp. pepper

1 Tbsp. vinegar

1 Tbsp. brown sugar

½ cup ketchup

1 Tbsp. Worcestershire sauce

Brown ground beef and onion in a heavy saucepan. Add wheat, lentils, water, tomatoes, salt, pepper, vinegar, brown sugar, ketchup, and Worcestershire sauce. Cover and cook slowly for 2–3 hours. Thin with water or tomato juice if desired.

Barley, Rice, and Lentil Soup

Yield: 9 to 10 cups

2 (14-oz.) cans chicken stock

1 (14-oz.) can diced tomatoes

3 cups water

⅓ cup pearled barley

⅓ cup brown rice

⅓ cup lentils

1 tsp. minced garlic

1 tsp. chicken bouillon

1 onion, chopped, or 2 Tbsp.
   dry chopped onion

2 carrots, chopped

1 stalk celery, chopped

1 tsp. basil

salt to taste

1 Tbsp. cider vinegar

Combine chicken stock, tomatoes, water, barley, rice, lentils, garlic, bouillon, onion, carrots, celery, basil, and salt in heavy saucepan. Bring to a boil. Cover, reduce heat, and simmer until grains are tender, about 45 minutes. Add vinegar and serve.

Tip: You can cook this in a slow cooker on low for 4–6 hours. Or cook in a pressure cooker for 20 minutes; remove from heat and let pressure down naturally.

Lentil Rice Stew

Yield: 6 servings

Double or triple this recipe to feed a large group. Yummy served with corn bread.

4 cups chicken broth, or water with chicken bouillon added

1 cup dry lentils

½ cup brown rice

1 large onion, chopped, or 2 Tbsp. dry chopped onion

1 tsp. basil

½ tsp. oregano

1 Tbsp. minced garlic or ½ tsp. garlic powder

1 tsp. salt

grated cheese

In large heavy saucepan, add broth, lentils, rice, onion, basil, oregano, garlic, and salt. (If desired, mince onion in blender with 1 cup of the water beforehand.) Bring to a boil. Let simmer for 45–60 minutes, or until water is absorbed. Top with grated cheese and serve.

Corn Chowder

Yield: 6 to 8 servings

A great favorite on the East Coast.

2 potatoes

1 onion, chopped, or 2 Tbsp. dry chopped onion

1 Tbsp. oil

1 tsp. salt

⅛ tsp. pepper

½ tsp. marjoram

2 (14-oz.) cans cream-style corn; or 2 cans corn with liquid, lightly blended

1 (14-oz.) can cream of celery soup, optional

4 cups milk, or 1 cup dry milk and 4 cups water

1–2 Tbsp. dry potato flakes, optional

Precook potatoes in the microwave for 5–6 minutes or until soft. Let cool slightly and dice. In medium saucepan, mix potatoes, onion, salt, pepper, marjoram, corn, celery soup, and milk. If using dry milk, mix water and dry milk in blender before adding to soup. Heat but do not boil, 12–15 minutes. If a thicker soup is desired, stir in 1–2 tablespoons dry potato flakes.

Dry Onion Soup Mix

This equals one package of dry onion soup mix.

**1 Tbsp. instant beef
    bouillon granules**

2 Tbsp. instant minced onion

½ tsp. onion powder

Mix all ingredients. Store in airtight container.

Dry Soup Mix

Yield: 12 cups mix

Add a cup of this dry soup mix to any soup or stew. It's very good and is a nutritious way to extend almost any soup. Add water as needed.

2 cups raw pearled barley

2 cups lentils

2 cups brown or white rice

2 cups macaroni

2 cups split peas

2 cups dry chopped onion

Mix ingredients. Store in large covered container in cool place.

GF Cream Soup Mix

Yield: 3½ cups dry mix equals 10 cans cream soup

A fat-free dry mix that can be used in place of creamed condensed soups in a variety of recipes. Keep the mix on hand for convenience. It adds a rich, creamy flavor to any cream soup, casserole, creamed vegetables, gravies, and so on, and it is an easy way to utilize and rotate dry milk. The mix is gluten-free.

2 cups dry milk

1 cup cornstarch

**¼ cup gluten-free chicken
    bouillon granules**

2 Tbsp. dry chopped onion

¼ tsp. pepper

Combine all ingredients and store in airtight container or closed plastic bag. Mix does not need to be refrigerated. Tape or write a how-to-use recipe (see next page) on the outside of container.

Cream Soup From Mix

Yield: 1¼ cups; about 1 can condensed cream soup

⅓ cup dry GF Cream Soup Mix   **1–2 Tbsp. butter or oil, optional**
  (p. 109)

1¼ cups water

Whisk soup mix and water together until blended. Add butter if desired. Cook and stir on stovetop or in microwave until thickened. Add mixture to recipe as you would a can of condensedcream soup. Or make any of the adaptations listed below.

Creamed Soup Adaptations

Make a double recipe if desired. Thin with milk or water if needed, or stir in 1–2 tablespoons dry potato flakes to thicken. Add spices if desired.

Add any of the following ingredients to the recipe above:

Cream of Chicken Soup: ½ cup diced cooked chicken

Cream of Mushroom Soup: 1 (4-oz.) can mushrooms, drained, chopped

Cream of Celery Soup: ½ cup cooked chopped celery

Cream of Broccoli or Cauliflower Soup: 1 cup cooked chopped florets

Cream of Asparagus Soup: 1 cup steamed chopped asparagus

Cream of Potato Soup: 1 cup cooked potato cubes

Creamed Vegetables: Cooked carrots, green beans, peas, etc.

Creamed Tuna or Creamed Chicken: 1 (5-oz.) can tuna or chicken. Serve over hot biscuits, noodles, or potatoes.

CHAPTER 6

Luscious Lunches

» SALADS AND DRESSINGS

Chicken Rice Salad

Yield: 10 to 12 servings

This salad is as tasty as it is beautiful. Just add hot rolls and yumm!

2 cups cubed cooked chicken

1 (20-oz.) can crushed pineapple, drained

3 cups cooked rice, brown or white

3 Tbsp. apple cider vinegar

¼ cup oil

3 Tbsp. brown sugar

1 tsp. salt

1 cup celery, finely diced

½ cup chopped green pepper

½ cup chopped red pepper

¾ cup light mayonnaise

1 cup red or green seedless grapes

1 (10-oz.) can mandarin oranges, drained

1 cup roasted, salted cashews, optional

Combine chicken, pineapple, and rice. Mix vinegar, oil, brown sugar, and salt and stir into chicken mixture. Cover and refrigerate overnight. Just before serving, stir in celery, green and red pepper, and mayonnaise. Gently fold in grapes and mandarin oranges. Add cashews if desired. Serve on lettuce leaf or croissant.

Barbecue Chicken Salad

Yield: 4 servings

A satisfying and delicious main meal salad.

2–3 cups shredded cooked chicken breast

¼–½ cup barbecue sauce (to taste)

4 warm flour tortillas

2–3 cups warm cooked rice

2 cups warm black beans

2–3 cups romaine lettuce, torn

2 tomatoes, finely diced, and 4 green onions, sliced

guacamole

corn chips

sour cream, optional

Spicy Ranch Dressing (below)

Simmer cooked chicken and barbecue sauce for 10–12 minutes. On each tortilla, layer rice, beans, chicken, lettuce, and tomato-onion mix. Add a side of guacamole and put crushed corn chips on top. Serve with sour cream, if desired, and Spicy Ranch Dressing.

Spicy Ranch Dressing

Yield: 2 cups

Serve as a dressing for salads or with chips.

1 cup ranch dressing

1 cup salsa

Mix ingredients well and refrigerate.

Chicken Salad

Yield: 4 cups

This is a very popular recipe to serve in croissants or rolls for almost any special occasion.

3 cups cooked diced chicken breast, or 2 (12-oz.) cans chicken breast, diced, with broth

½ cup finely diced celery

¼ cup finely diced onion

½ tsp. salt

½ cup mayonnaise

Combine chicken, celery, onion, salt, and mayonnaise. Mix well. You can add more or less mayonnaise, depending on your preference.

Fruit Salad

Yield: 10 to 12 servings

Crisp and chewy.

1 (15-oz.) can fruit cocktail

1 (11-oz.) can mandarin oranges

1 (15-oz.) can pineapple tidbits

2 apples, diced

3–4 bananas, sliced

1 cup cooked wheat, optional

1 cup cream, whipped, or 1 pkg. Dream Whip, prepared as directed

Drain fruit cocktail, oranges, and pineapple; reserve pineapple juice. Dip diced apples and banana slices in pineapple juice for 2–3 minutes to prevent darkening. Combine drained fruits, apples, bananas, wheat, and whipped cream or Dream Whip. Chill for 2 hours before serving.

Fresh Fruit Salad

Enjoy this delicious and nutritious salad.

1 orange, diced

1 cup pineapple tidbits, reserve juice

1 large unpeeled apple, diced

3–4 bananas, sliced

1 cup strawberries, sliced

1 cup grapes or other seasonal fruit

½ cup pecans

1 cup peach yogurt or Fruit Salad Dressing (below)

Mix orange and pineapple pieces and a little juice in large bowl. Stir in diced apple and banana slices, coating pieces with juice. Add strawberries, grapes or other seasonal fruit, and pecans. Fold in yogurt or Fruit Salad Dressing. Cover and refrigerate or serve immediately.

Fruit Salad Dressing

Yield: 6 to 10 servings

This dressing complements any fruit salad.

2 Tbsp. cornstarch

¼ cup sugar or honey

pinch of salt

1 cup apple, pineapple, or orange juice

In saucepan, whisk cornstarch, sugar, and salt into fruit juice. Bring to a boil, stirring constantly. Cook for 1–2 minutes, until thick and clear. Cool slightly. Thin with more juice if desired.

Snappy Fruit Salad Dressing

A favorite that couldn't be easier.

1 cup peach, strawberry, or vanilla yogurt

Drizzle over sliced fruit or fold into fruit salad.

Gazpacho Salad

Yield: 6 to 8 servings

A favorite garden salad that complements any summer meal.

2–3 cups diced tomatoes or cherry tomatoes cut in half

2 medium cucumbers, peeled and diced

½ red onion, finely chopped

1 tsp. basil

½ cup salsa or picante sauce

2–3 Tbsp. Italian dressing

Combine tomatoes, cucumbers, onion, and basil. Mix salsa and Italian dressing and pour over vegetables. Mix lightly and chill before serving.

Potato Salad

Yield: 12 servings

This is our very favorite—perfect every time!

6 large potatoes, boiled in skin

3–4 large hard-cooked eggs

1 small onion, chopped

2 dill pickles, finely chopped

1 cup salad dressing or mayonnaise

1 tsp. mustard

1–2 tsp. sugar or honey (to taste)

1 tsp. apple cider vinegar

1 tsp. salt

Peel and cube potatoes. Dice eggs and add to potatoes. Add onion and pickle and toss gently. Mix salad dressing or mayo, mustard, sugar or honey, vinegar, and salt in another bowl. Thin with milk or water to desired consistency. Pour over salad and mix lightly. Chill well before serving, 3–4 hours.

Taco Salad

Yield: 6 to 8 servings

Adding beans and rice adds flavor and nutrition to this favorite salad.

½ lb. lean ground beef

1–2 Tbsp. taco seasoning mix

1 (14-oz.) can pinto or
  kidney beans, with liquid

1 cup cooked rice

1 head lettuce, torn small

½ cup chopped ripe olives

1–2 cups shredded cheese

3–4 tomatoes, diced

1 small onion, finely chopped

salad dressing of choice

3–4 cups corn tortilla chips,
  slightly crushed

salsa

Brown ground beef in large skillet. Drain and discard fat. Add taco seasoning mix and beans. Simmer uncovered for 10–15 minutes. Stir in rice and let cool for 8–10 minutes. Mix lettuce, olives, cheese, tomatoes, and onion in large bowl. Toss with favorite salad dressing. Add meat mixture and slightly crushed tortilla chips just before serving. Toss lightly and serve immediately with salsa.

Crispy Coleslaw

Yield: 6 to 8 servings

A refreshing, tasty treat.

½ head cabbage,
  shredded, or 1 bag
  coleslaw mix

2 carrots, shredded

⅓–½ cup Italian Dressing

½ tsp. celery seed

½ tsp. dill weed

¼ cup sunflower seeds

Mix cabbage or coleslaw mix and carrots. Combine Italian Dressing, celery seed, and dill weed. Stir into coleslaw mix. Sprinkle with sunflower seeds. Serve immediately or cover and chill. Keeps well.

Caesar Salad

Yield: 4 to 6 servings

So delicious and so easy.

½ cup olive oil or canola oil

1 clove garlic, peeled

2 Tbsp. fresh lemon juice

1 tsp. Worcestershire sauce

½ tsp. salt

¼ tsp. pepper

1 egg

1 large head romaine
    lettuce, torn (6–8 cups)

1 cup croutons

½ cup parmesan cheese

Put olive oil, garlic, lemon juice, Worcestershire sauce, salt, and pepper into a blender. Bring a small saucepan of water to a boil and adjust heat so it bubbles gently. Use a spoon to lower egg into the pot and cook for 60–90 seconds. Remove egg with a slotted spoon. Let it cool just enough to handle, then crack into a bowl and scoop out the white that clings to the shell and add egg to blender ingredients. Blend lightly, just until well mixed. Pour over lettuce and toss well. Top with croutons and parmesan and then toss salad once more at the table. Serve immediately.

Tip: For a Caesar salad main course, toss a can of drained salmon or tuna into the dressing. Or top the tossed salad with shredded chicken breast

Creamy Coleslaw

Yield: 8 to 10 servings

The dressing gives this salad that wonderful old-fashioned flavor.

½ **head cabbage, shredded, or
4–5 cups coleslaw mix**

½ **green pepper, diced**

1 **carrot, peeled and shredded**

½ **cup crushed pineapple,
optional**

½ **cup salad dressing of choice**

½ **tsp. mustard**

2–4 **Tbsp. sugar (to taste)**

1 **tsp. apple cider vinegar**

salt to taste

Combine cabbage, green pepper, carrot, and optional pineapple in serving bowl. Mix mayonnaise or salad dressing, mustard, sugar, vinegar, and salt in small bowl. If too thick, thin with a little water. Add dressing to salad and mix well. Serve immediately or chill and serve.

Pickled Cucumbers

Yield: 10 to 12 servings

Summer eating isn't complete without fresh pickled cucumbers.

3–4 **cups cucumbers, peeled or
unpeeled**

1 **small onion**

½ **tsp. salt**

pepper to taste

½ **cup water**

½ **cup cider vinegar**

1–2 **tsp. sugar (to taste)**

Slice cucumbers and onion quite thin. Sprinkle liberally with salt and pepper and mix in carefully. Let cucumbers "weep" for 30 minutes or so. Drain liquid. Barely cover with mixture of water, vinegar, and sugar. Cover and chill for 30–60 minutes before serving.

Chicken Pasta Salad

Yield: 10 to 12 servings

Quick and flavorful.

1 (10-oz.) pkg. spiral pasta

1 large red onion, diced

3 stalks celery, thinly sliced

1 large cucumber, peeled and
  diced

2 cups diced tomatoes

2 cups cooked diced chicken

1 cup red wine vinegar salad
  dressing

Cook pasta as directed on package, rinse with cold water, and drain.
Gently fold in onion, celery, cucumber, tomatoes, and chicken. Pour
dressing over ingredients. Mix carefully. Refrigerate for 2–3 hours
before serving.

Carrot Salad

Yield: 6 to 8 servings

A colorful addition to most any meal.

4 carrots, peeled and finely
  shredded

1 cup crushed pineapple

¼ cup raisins

1–2 Tbsp. sugar

2–4 Tbsp. salad dressing

Combine shredded carrots, pineapple, and raisins. Mix sugar and
salad dressing and stir in. Cover and chill well before serving, for
1–2 hours.

Pasta Salad

Yield: 12 servings

This tasty salad feeds a crowd.

1 (12-oz.) pkg. small elbow macaroni or any favorite pasta

4 hard-cooked eggs, diced

1 bunch green onions, chopped

1 cup diced cheese

1 (10-oz.) frozen petite peas, thawed but not cooked
1–1½ cups salad dressing or mayonnaise

1 tsp. salt

½ tsp. celery salt

½ tsp. onion powder

½ tsp. garlic powder

1 tsp. mustard

1 Tbsp. sugar

1 Tbsp. vinegar

Cook macaroni as directed on package, rinse with cold water, and drain. Place in large bowl. Add eggs, onion, cheese, and peas. Toss gently. In another bowl mix salad dressing or mayo, salt, celery salt, onion powder, garlic powder, mustard, sugar, and vinegar. Thin with water if needed. Pour dressing over salad just before serving and mix lightly.

Honey Mustard Salad Dressing

Yield: ³/₄ cup

A refreshing mix of herbs and seasonings that make a favorite dressing.

½ cup mayonnaise

¼ cup honey

2 Tbsp. dijon mustard

Combine all ingredients in medium bowl. Cover and chill to store.

Cooked Salad Dressing

Yield: 1 ½ cups

A flavorful dressing for potato salad, pasta salad, coleslaw, tuna, or bean salad.

2 Tbsp. sugar

2 Tbsp. flour

1 tsp. dry mustard

1 tsp. salt

dash of pepper

1 egg, slightly beaten

1 cup milk or water

¼ cup vinegar

2 Tbsp. butter

Mix sugar, flour, dry mustard, salt, and pepper in medium saucepan. Whisk in egg and milk or water and mix well. Slowly stir in vinegar. Cook over medium heat, stirring constantly, until mixture thickens, about 5 minutes. Remove from heat and stir in butter. Cover and store in refrigerator. This is a concentrate. To use, dilute with canned milk, milk, or water to desired consistency.

French Dressing

Yield: 2 cups

One of the best French dressings we've tasted.

1 cup salad oil

½ cup catsup

⅓ cup red wine vinegar or cider vinegar

2–3 Tbsp. sugar or honey

1 tsp. garlic salt

½ tsp. onion powder

Combine all ingredients in a blender or food processor, or put into a glass jar and shake well. Refrigerate. Dressing keeps well.

Vinaigrette Salad Dressing

Yield: about 1 cup

Light and flavorful.

½ cup cider vinegar

¼ cup oil

1–2 Tbsp. sugar

¼ tsp. salt

½ tsp. mustard

½ tsp. celery or dillseed

Combine ingredients in a jar. Shake well and chill.

Poppy Seed Dressing

Yield: 1 cup

Low-fat and tasty.

⅓ cup red wine vinegar or cider vinegar

⅓ cup water

¼ cup olive oil

1 Tbsp. dijon mustard

3 Tbsp. sugar

1 tsp. poppy seeds

1 tsp. onion salt

Whisk or blend all ingredients. Chill before serving.

Vegetable Dip

Yield: 2 cups

This dip is easy to make and adds zest to all raw vegetables.

1 cup mayonnaise

1 cup sour cream, or cottage cheese, blended

2–3 tsp. dry chopped onion

1–2 tsp. dill weed or dillseed

1 tsp. seasoned salt

Mix ingredients well and chill at least 1 hour before serving.

Guacamole

Yield: 4 servings

Quick and delicious.

2 large ripe avocados

1–2 Tbsp. fresh lime or lemon juice

2–3 Tbsp. salsa

corn chips or tortilla chips, optional

Mash avocados in small bowl using a fork. Add lime juice and salsa, stirring just until combined. Serve immediately with chips.

Hummus

Yield: 2 cups

Use as a dip or sandwich spread.

1 (14-oz.) can garbanzo or white beans

2–3 Tbsp. tahini (sesame butter), or 3 Tbsp. raw sesame seeds

2–3 Tbsp. lemon juice (to taste)

1 Tbsp. diced onion

1 Tbsp. minced garlic

½ tsp. cumin

¼ tsp. salt

Drain beans and reserve liquid. Put beans, tahini or sesame seeds, lemon juice, onion, garlic, cumin, salt, and ⅓–½ cup bean liquid in blender or food processor. Blend until smooth, adding additional liquid if desired. Refrigerate.

GROW YOUR OWN SPROUTS

Sprouts have long been called our most perfect living food because they are fresh, uncontaminated, and power-packed with nutrients. You can grow a new crop in three to five days, no matter what the climate or where you live. Alfalfa, mung beans, wheat, and sunflower seeds are some of the most popular seeds for home sprouting. For safe, trouble-free sprouting, invest in a small plastic sprouter. Always buy sprouting seeds—these are untreated and have a high germination rate.

For perfect sprouts:

1. Soak seeds in pure room-temperature water. Soak small seeds for 8–12 hours or overnight; soak larger seeds, such as wheat, for 18–24 hours. Allow 3–4 times more water than seeds. Try these amounts to begin with:

Alfalfa and related seeds: 2 tablespoons, 1 cup water

Mung beans, lentils, and other beans: $1/2$ cup, 2 cups water

Sunflower seeds: $1/2$ cup, 2 cups water

Wheat, rye, oats, and related grains: $1/2$ cup, 2 cups water

2. After soaking, pour seeds into a sprouter and drain well. Or put seeds into a widemouth quart or gallon jar and cover the jar mouth with a clean piece of gauze or knee-high nylon hose to facilitate draining the water after rinsing. Lay bottle on its side for better ventilation during sprouting. Since sprouts grow best in the dark, keep your "garden" covered with a light towel and out of direct sunlight. Keep them in a conspicuous place so you won't forget to rinse often. Don't cover with a lid because they need oxygen.

3. Rinse and drain sprouts morning, noon (if possible), and night. Fill sink with several inches of room-temperature water, immerse sprouter, and move up and down to thoroughly rinse seeds. Drain well by tilting the sprouter slightly. Extra rinsing keeps alfalfa and mung bean sprouts mild and crisp. You can control the growth of your sprouts to some degree by varying the rinse water temperature. Cold water slows their growth, warm water accelerates it, and heavily chlorinated water may kill sprouts before they get a chance to grow!

4. Sprouts are ready to eat in 2–5 days. Sample them often to see when they taste best to you. Each seed and grain has its peak of quality. Sunflower seeds are crunchy-tender in just 24 hours. Wheat tastes best when the sprout is the same length as the seed, which takes approximately 48 hours. Mung beans and lentils are at their taste peak when they are ¼–1 inch long, which usually takes 2–3 days. Alfalfa grows 1–1½ inches long in 4–5 days. Uncover alfalfa on the last day so it will turn green.

5. When sprouts are ready to eat, rinse with cold water to stop their growth. Eat immediately or store in a covered container in the refrigerator.

» SANDWICH CREATIONS

Chicken Sandwich Filling

Yield: 2 cups

Satisfying and nutritious.

1–1½ cups cooked diced chicken or turkey, or 2 (5-oz.) cans chicken or turkey, with liquid

½ cup cooked brown rice

1 stalk celery, finely diced, optional

¼ cup salad dressing or mayonnaise

Mix all ingredients together. Chill thoroughly.

Chicken-Rice Spread

Yield: 5 to 6 cups

This juicy filling is delicious in sandwiches, pita bread, and stuffed tomatoes.

1 cup cooked brown or white rice

2 cups canned or cooked diced chicken or turkey

2–3 hard-boiled eggs, chopped

2 small tomatoes, diced

½ cup crushed pineapple, drained

1 avocado, peeled and chopped

½ cup finely shredded cheese

¾ cup mayonnaise

1 Tbsp. dijon-style mustard

¼ tsp. celery salt

½ tsp. pepper

Combine all ingredients. Stir carefully and only enough to moisten ingredients. Cover and chill well, 1 hour, or serve immediately. This spread freezes well.

Egg Salad Sandwich Filling

Yield: 1¹/₂ cups

Quick and easy.

3 eggs, hard-cooked

¼ tsp. mustard

¼ tsp. salt (to taste)

2–3 Tbsp. salad dressing or mayonnaise

Mash or finely chop eggs. Add mustard, salt, and salad dressing or mayonnaise. Mix well. Chill.

Tuna Sandwich Filling

Yield: about 1 cup

An old favorite takes on a new twist.

1–2 cans tuna in water, reserve liquid

½ cup cooked rice

½ stalk celery, finely chopped, optional

1–2 hard-cooked eggs, finely diced, optional

1–2 Tbsp. pickle relish or diced pickle

¼–¹/₃ cup mayonnaise or salad dressing

Mix tuna, rice, celery, eggs, pickle relish, and mayonnaise or salad dressing, using liquid as needed to moisten filling. Cover and chill.

Bean Wrap

Yield: 4 servings

Very satisfying and tasty.

2 cups warm refried beans	1 small avocado, diced, optional
¼ cup diced onion	lettuce, diced
½ cup shredded cheese	2 (10-inch) tortillas, warmed
½ tomato, diced	salsa or mild taco sauce

Layer warm beans, onion, cheese, tomato, avocado, and lettuce on tortillas, dividing equally. Add salsa to taste. Fold ends of tortilla in, roll up to completely enclose filling, cut in half, and serve.

CHAPTER 7

Delicious Dinners

Enjoy the family unity that eating together brings. Our approach saves time and money, and planning ahead is the key. As you begin eating more basic foods, an improvement in health, plus lower grocery bills, will soon be evident. You can do this without spending all day in the kitchen. Cook once and eat twice or more by preparing larger quantities and freezing some for later. Many tasty one-dish meals are included here, which speeds food preparation and cleanup. The recipes are quick, are easy to prepare, and have been family tested. They are good and good for you! Eat from your garden and orchard whenever possible. If your meal is well-balanced, your plate will be a rainbow of color.

» Pressure-Cooking: A Big Time-Saver

Pressure cookers are a quick and efficient way to cook food. They are safe to use and save time and fuel, taking only about one-third the usual cooking time. Keep in mind that several sizes and types of pressure cookers are available, so shop carefully for one that fits your needs. Choose a quality pot with heat-resistant handles, a locking lid that is easy to maneuver, and a heavy bottom.

Pressure cookers are ideal for foods that normally require a long cooking time, such as soups, stews, meats, vegetables, rice, and beans. Pressure cookers not only tenderize tough meat and old beans, but they also keep the flavor and nutrients within, producing a tastier, healthier meal in just minutes, not hours. Be familiar with the owner's manual for your own pressure cooker and follow the guidelines carefully.

Slow Cooker Tips

Most main dishes can be cooked using a slow cooker. With a little practice, you'll become an expert. General instructions are included below.

All-day cooking..........................Low, 8–12 hours

Half-day cooking ....High, 4-6 hours

If morning time is limited, prepare meat and clean and cut vegetables the night before. Refrigerate until morning.

When cooking meat and vegetable combinations, place vegetables in the bottom. The liquid helps them cook and improves flavor. You can sprinkle vegetables with quick-cooking tapioca if desired. It's a great thickener for slow-cooking use because it needs no stirring and does not lump. Top with meat.

Sweet-and-Sour Chicken

Yield: 6 servings

This one-dish meal is ready in minutes

Menu: Steamed broccoli, relish tray

1 cup pineapple tidbits

1 large green pepper, diced

1 small onion, diced, or 1 Tbsp.
dry chopped onion

2 Tbsp. oil

1 cup chicken broth or
1 bouillon cube and 1 cup
hot water

2 Tbsp. soy sauce

3 Tbsp. vinegar

¼ cup brown sugar

pinch of salt

2 Tbsp. cornstarch

¼ cup water

2 cups cooked cubed chicken or
1 (14-oz.) can chicken, cubed,
with liquid

3–4 cups hot cooked rice

Drain pineapple and save juice. In large skillet, sauté green pepper, onion, and pineapple in hot oil for 3–4 minutes. Add pineapple juice, broth or bouillon, soy sauce, vinegar, brown sugar, and salt. Stir cornstarch into water and add to mixture. Cook and stir gently until thickened. Add chicken and heat through. Serve over hot rice.

Chicken Divan

Yield: 5 to 6 servings

Good eating for family or guests.

Menu: Frozen corn and green salad

2 cups broccoli

3 cups cooked rice (1 cup uncooked)

½ cup mayonnaise

2 Tbsp. lemon juice

1 (10-oz.) can cream of chicken soup

2–3 cups cooked chicken, cubed, or canned chicken, drained and cubed

buttered bread crumbs, optional

Preheat oven to 375°F. Steam broccoli for 4–6 minutes, or until barely tender. In a bowl, combine cooked rice, mayonnaise, and lemon juice. Spread rice mixture evenly on the bottom of a 9×13 baking dish. Arrange broccoli and chicken on top of rice mixture. Cover with soup. Top with bread crumbs if desired. Bake until hot and bubbly, 15–20 minutes, or microwave on high for 8–10 minutes.

Chicken Cacciatore

Yield: 4 servings

Easy-to-prepare chicken with a change of flavor.

Menu: Baked squash, green beans

4 chicken pieces	½ tsp. oregano
salt and pepper	1 tsp. sugar
flour	parmesan cheese, optional
2 Tbsp. oil	3 cups hot cooked rice
2 Tbsp. minced garlic	
1 (14-oz.) can stewed tomatoes, mild salsa, or meatless spaghetti sauce	

Season chicken with salt and pepper and then coat with flour. In skillet, brown chicken in oil. Sprinkle garlic over chicken. Add stewed tomatoes and sprinkle with oregano and sugar. Cover and simmer for 20–30 minutes. Remove chicken to platter. Sprinkle parmesan cheese on sauce before serving over rice.

Chicken Dinner in a Pot

Yield: 6 to 8 servings

A delicious one-dish meal. Use oven or slow-cooker, or simmer on the stove.

Menu: Creamy coleslaw, sliced tomatoes

1 (3- to 4-lb.) whole chicken, or
   6–8 pieces chicken, skinned

6 potatoes, cut in half

20 baby carrots or 6 carrots, cut

2 onions, sliced

salt and pepper

poultry seasoning, or seasoned
   salt

Preheat oven to 350°F. Wash chicken and place in roasting pan or roasting bag. Arrange vegetables around chicken. Sprinkle chicken and vegetables with salt, pepper, and poultry seasoning or seasoned salt. Cover and bake for about 1½ hours, until tender, or as directed on roasting bag.

Tip: For slow cooker, cook on low for 6–8 hours, high for 4–6 hours. Or you can simmer on the stove for 45–60 minutes.

Hawaiian Haystacks

Yield: 4 to 6 servings

This favorite buffet-style meal is fun for children and adults.

Menu: Hot biscuits or rolls

2–3 cups chicken gravy, or 1 (10-oz.) can cream of chicken soup and ½ soup can milk or water

2 cups diced canned or cooked chicken or turkey

3–4 cups hot cooked rice, brown or white

1 cup grated cheese

3 stalks celery, diced

6 green onions, finely sliced, or 1 onion, diced

3 tomatoes, chopped

1 green bell pepper, chopped

1 cup crushed pineapple or tidbits

1 cup shredded coconut

1 cup slivered almonds

1–2 cups Chinese noodles

Cook rice. Heat gravy. Add chicken or turkey. Prepare remaining ingredients. Place each in a separate container and serve buffet style. Start with the rice. Add chicken and gravy, cheese, celery, onions, tomatoes, green pepper, pineapple, coconut, and almonds. Build yourself a "stack" and top it with a sprinkle of Chinese noodles.

Salsa Chicken 'n' Rice

Yield: 5 to 6 Servings

Menu: Broccoli and cauliflower, green salad

1–3 lbs. boneless skinless chicken

2 cups salsa or picante sauce

1–2 Tbsp. sugar, to taste

3–4 cups cooked rice

Cook chicken, salsa, and sugar in slow cooker on low for 5–6 hours, or on high for 2–3 hours, until chicken shreds easily with a fork. Shred chicken into salsa. Thin with water if needed. Serve over rice or see "Tip" below.

Tip: No salsa or picante sauce? Use canned tomatoes and season with chili powder, taco seasoning and sugar. Or use Mexican stewed tomatoes

Chicken and Dumplings

Yield: 6 servings

Enjoy these tender, light dumplings.

Menu: Broccoli, raw vegetable plate

6 pieces chicken, skinned	**1 tsp. salt**
1 onion, chopped, or 1–2 Tbsp. dry chopped onion	**water**

Dumplings:

2 cups flour	**3 Tbsp. oil**
1 Tbsp. baking powder	**1 scant cup milk, or ¼ cup dry milk and 1 scant cup water**
1 tsp. salt	

Wash chicken. Place in large pan with onion, salt, and just enough water to cover. Bring to a boil and simmer gently until tender, 20–25 minutes. Mix flour, baking powder, and salt. If using dry milk, add to dry ingredients. Add oil and milk or water. Stir with fork just until mixed. Drop by spoonfuls onto chicken in boiling broth. Cover and let simmer for 15 minutes without lifting lid. Thicken broth to make gravy if desired.

Chicken and Noodles

Yield: 6 to 8 servings

A favorite dish.

Menu: Frozen petite peas, sliced tomatoes

6–8 pieces chicken, skinned

6–8 cups water

1 Tbsp. dry chopped onion

2 carrots, diced

1–2 tsp. salt (to taste)

2–3 cups noodles

Place chicken, water, onion, carrots, and salt in large saucepan. Bring to a boil. Simmer chicken for 20–30 minutes or until tender. Let cool slightly in broth. Remove chicken from bones, leaving meat in large pieces. Add chicken pieces and noodles to broth. Simmer for 10–12 minutes or until noodles are tender. Serve over mashed potatoes if desired.

Pork or Chicken Sandwich

Yield: 3 to 4 servings

You can't beat the convenience and taste.

1 (14-oz.) can pork or chicken pieces, with liquid

¼ cup salsa

2–3 Tbsp. brown sugar

¼ tsp. salt

Place pork or chicken in saucepan. Stir in salsa, brown sugar, and salt. Bring to a boil and let simmer uncovered for 10–12 minutes. Shred meat slightly with fork if desired. Serve on buns or over baked potatoes or rice.

Chicken Broccoli Casserole

Yield: 8 to 10 servings

A scrumptious way to use canned chicken or turkey.

Menu: Baked beans, corn, green salad

1 (6-oz.) pkg. chicken stuffing mix, or use Stuffing Recipe (below)

1 (10-oz.) can cream of chicken soup

½ cup sour cream, optional

1 soup can chicken broth, milk, or water

2–3 cups cooked broccoli florets

2–3 cups canned or cooked chicken, cubed

½ cup fine bread crumbs, optional

Preheat oven to 350°F. Prepare stuffing mix as directed on package. Mix soup with optional sour cream and broth, milk, or water. Steam broccoli until barely tender and drain. Cover bottom of 9×13 baking dish with a thin layer of soup mix and spread half the stuffing over soup. Layer the cooked chicken and then the broccoli. Spread remaining stuffing on top of broccoli. Pour soup mix over all. Sprinkle lightly with bread crumbs if desired. Bake uncovered until hot and bubbly, 30 minutes.

Stuffing Recipe

4–5 cups dry bread cubes or crumbled corn bread

1 tsp. poultry seasoning or sage

1 tsp. salt

dash of pepper

1–2 Tbsp. dry chopped onion

2 Tbsp. butter or margarine

½–¾ cup hot water

In large bowl, mix bread cubes or corn bread, poultry seasoning or sage, salt, and pepper. Stir onion and butter into hot water. Pour over bread mixture and toss to mix well. Cover and let it stand for 5–8 minutes.

Barbecue Shredded Chicken, Beef, or Pork

Yield: 18 to 20 servings

This recipe feeds a crowd and can easily be doubled or tripled.

Menu: Potato salad, veggie tray

6–8 lbs. boneless chicken, beef, or pork

water

1 Tbsp. liquid smoke

1–2 cups barbecue sauce (to taste)

2–4 Tbsp. honey (to taste), optional

Wash meat and place in slow cooker or large heavy saucepan. Barely cover with water and add liquid smoke. Cover slow cooker and cook on low for 8–10 hours, or simmer on stove until meat is very tender. Drain and save cooking liquid from meat. Shred meat with forks. Slowly add barbecue sauce, starting with ½ cup. Add honey if desired, which mellows out the barbecue sauce. Add cooking liquid from meat to desired consistency. Serve on buns.

Creamed Tuna or Chicken

Yield: 6 to 8 servings

The best creamed tuna ever! Serve over toast, hot biscuits, favorite pasta, or steamed wheat.

Menu: Broccoli, corn, green salad

2 Tbsp. butter

¼ cup flour

½ tsp. salt

pinch of pepper

1 tsp. dry chopped onion

½ tsp. chicken bouillon

2 cups milk, or ½ cup dry milk and 2 cups water

2 (5-oz.) cans tuna or chicken, drained and diced

In medium saucepan, melt butter. Blend in flour, salt, pepper, onion, and bouillon. Add milk (or water with dry milk) all at once and cook quickly, stirring constantly until thick. Stir in tuna or chicken and serve over toast, hot biscuits, or pasta.

Salmon Burgers

Yield: 8 to 10 servings

Makes tasty sandwich fillings.

Menu: Creamed peas and potatoes, beets, fresh vegetables

1 (15-oz.) can salmon, with liquid

1 egg, slightly beaten

1 cup soft bread crumbs or cracker crumbs

¼ cup water or milk

2 tsp. dry chopped onion or 4–5 green onions, chopped

1 Tbsp. lemon juice

pinch of salt and pepper

Remove and discard skin and bones from salmon. Flake salmon with fork. Do not drain. In bowl with salmon, add egg, bread crumbs, water or milk, onion, lemon juice, and salt and pepper and mix well. Shape into patties or drop spoonfuls onto hot nonstick griddle. Cook until golden on each side. Don't overcook.

Salmon Loaf: Preheat oven to 350°F. Press mixture into medium-size greased loaf pan or 1-quart baking dish. Bake uncovered for 30 minutes or just until done.

Cheesy Potatoes

Yield: 16 to 18 servings

This popular recipe is often served at funeral dinners.

Menu: Ham, savory baked beans, green salad

8–10 large potatoes, boiled, or 30 oz. frozen hash brown potatoes, or 4 cups dried potato shreds soaked for 30 minutes in hot water and drained

2 (10-oz.) cans cream of chicken soup

2 cups sour cream

1 large onion, finely chopped, or 2 Tbsp. dry chopped onion

1–2 cups shredded cheese

1 tsp. salt

dash of pepper

1 cup crushed cornflakes or bread crumbs

2 Tbsp. melted butter

Preheat oven to 350°F. Peel and grate, or finely dice, cooked potatoes; or use thawed hash brown potatoes; or use dehydrated potato shreds, soaked and drained. In a large bowl, mix soup, sour cream, onion, cheese, salt, and pepper. Fold potatoes gently into sauce, mixing well. Place in large casserole dish or 9×13 baking dish. Mix crushed cornflakes or bread crumbs with melted butter and spread evenly over potatoes before baking. Cover and bake for 30 minutes. Uncover and bake for 10–20 more minutes or until hot and bubbly.

Tip: Casserole can be made ahead and refrigerated. When serving, bake an additional 10–15 minutes or until hot.

Tip: To make in a roaster oven, triple the recipe. Start oven at 325°F and then turn to 150°F.

Scalloped Potatoes

Yield: 8 to 10 servings

The seasonings make these potatoes taste extra special.

Serve with any meat dish.

6 large potatoes, peeled	½ tsp. paprika
3 Tbsp. butter	½ tsp. dry mustard
1 onion, chopped, or 2 Tbsp. dry chopped onion	¼ cup flour
1 tsp. salt	2 cups milk, or ½ cup dry milk and 2 cups water
⅛ tsp. pepper	½ cup shredded cheese

Preheat oven to 350°F. Cube or slice potatoes and place in large baking dish. Melt butter in saucepan. Add onion and sauté for 2–3 minutes. Stir in salt, pepper, paprika, dry mustard, and flour. If using dry milk, mix into dry ingredients. Whisk in milk or water and cook until thick, stirring constantly. Fold sauce gently into potatoes. Cover and bake until tender, 1 hour. Sprinkle with cheese and serve.

Tip: To cut baking time, microwave on high for 10–15 minutes and then bake in oven for 30–40 minutes or until potatoes are tender. Or boil cubed potatoes for 10–12 minutes while making sauce. Drain, add sauce, and bake until tender, about 30 minutes.

Ham and Scalloped Potatoes: Follow recipe above. Fold in 1–2 cups diced ham. Cover and bake as directed.

Potato Patties

Yield: 6 patties

Great way to use leftover mashed potatoes.

2 cups mashed potatoes
1 egg, slightly beaten

¼ cup chopped onion
pinch of salt and pepper

Combine potatoes, egg, onion, and salt and pepper and mix well. Shape into 6 patties or drop mixture by spoonfuls onto nonstick or lightly greased griddle. Cook until golden brown, about 4 minutes on each side.

Potato Hash

Yield: 4 servings

An excellent way to use leftover baked or boiled potatoes. Makes a quick meal.

½ lb. lean ground beef
1 large onion, diced
3–4 cooked potatoes, peeled and diced

salt and pepper to taste
1 (14-oz.) can whole kernel corn, optional

Brown ground beef and onion in nonstick skillet. Add potatoes and season with salt and pepper. Cook over medium heat until potatoes are slightly brown, stirring occasionally. Add corn and heat until it's hot.

Fried Potatoes and Onions

Yield: 3 to 4 servings

Have fun cooking a large quantity outdoors in a Dutch oven.

2–4 potatoes

2 Tbsp. oil

1 medium onion, chopped

salt and pepper to taste

Peel and slice or dice potatoes. Heat oil in nonstick frying pan. Add onion and potatoes and season with salt and pepper. Cook over medium heat until potatoes are slightly brown, stirring occasionally. Add 2 tablespoons water. Cover pan and steam until potatoes are tender. If using cooked potatoes, sauté onion in oil for 3–4 minutes, add potatoes, and cook until slightly brown and hot.

Savory Pot Roast

Yield: 8 to 10 servings

This one-dish meal is easy to prepare ahead of time and requires little cleanup.

1 (3- to 4-lb.) lean beef roast

garlic salt

pepper

flour

2 Tbsp. oil

1–2 large onions, sliced or chopped

6 medium potatoes, cut in half

6–8 carrots, cut in fourths

½ cup water

Preheat oven to 275°F–300°F. Season roast liberally with garlic salt and a dash of pepper and coat with flour. In heavy roasting pan, brown all sides of meat in hot oil for 10–15 minutes. Add onions, potatoes, carrots, and ½ cup water (unless adding vegetables later, as preferred). Sprinkle vegetables with garlic salt. Cover tightly and bake in preheated oven for 3–4 hours. (Or bake at 350°F for 2–2½ hours.) Add vegetables last hour if preferred.

Tip: You can place vegetables and browned roast in slow cooker. Cook on low for 10–12 hours or high for 4–6 hours. Roast can also be simmered slowly on top of the stove for 2–3 hours.

Corned Beef 'n' Cabbage Dinner

Yield: 6 servings

A memorable St. Patrick's Day meal. Very easy to prepare.

1 corned beef brisket, flat cut

water

1 spice packet, optional

6 carrots, peeled and cut in chunks

5 potatoes, peeled and cut in half

1 cabbage, cut in wedges

Wash brisket in cold water. Place in a large pot that's big enough to hold vegetables later. Add water to cover meat completely, but no more. Add spice packet if desired. Cover pot, bring to a boil, and simmer for about 3 hours. Remove meat to warm platter and cover with foil. Just before serving, slice meat thinly across the grain.

Add carrots and potatoes to the pot. Cover, bring to a boil, and cook for 10 minutes. Add cabbage and simmer for 20 more minutes, just until vegetables are tender. Dish everything up into bowls and serve.

Tip: Never add extra water to the pan before cooking vegetables—just use what has cooked down. Otherwise vegetables taste weak and diluted. They need the good corned beef flavor from the meat to season them.

Tip: Mash carrots and potatoes together on your plate. Add butter, salt, and pepper to taste. Sprinkle with apple cider vinegar. Cut up the cabbage and corned beef on top of that. Season again and enjoy. Simple and delicious!

Meat Loaf

Yield: 6 to 8 servings

Menu: Scalloped potatoes, steamed green beans, raw vegetables

3 slices bread, or 1 cup cracker crumbs or oats

1 (8-oz.) can tomato sauce or 1 cup milk

1 lb. lean ground beef

1 egg, slightly beaten

1 onion, finely minced, or 1 Tbsp. dry chopped onion

½ tsp. salt

½ tsp. pepper

1 (8-oz.) can tomato sauce

Preheat oven to 350°F. Break bread into small pieces and soak in tomato sauce or milk for 5 minutes. Add ground beef, egg, onion, salt, and pepper. Mix lightly but well. Place in loaf pan. Cover with tomato sauce and bake for 60 minutes.

Beef Stroganoff

Yield: 5 to 6 servings

Menu: Glazed Carrots, green salad

1 lb. sirloin or round steak or 1 lb. lean ground beef

oil

1 onion, diced

¼ cup flour

½ tsp. garlic salt

1 cup water

1 (4-oz.) can mushrooms, with liquid

1 (10-oz.) can cream of mushroom soup

1 cup sour cream, yogurt, or buttermilk

Trim fat from meat; cut steak diagonally across grain in strips ¼ inch wide—strips should be very thin. Heat a little oil in skillet and brown meat on medium-high heat. Add onion and sauté for 2–3 minutes. Stir in flour and garlic salt. Add water and mushrooms, including liquid. Stir in mushroom soup and heat until liquid boils. Simmer for 8–10 minutes. Just before serving, stir in sour cream, yogurt, or buttermilk. Serve over hot noodles, rice, or mashed potatoes.

Sloppy Joes

Yield: 10 to 12 servings

Everyone loves this old favorite.

Menu: Chips, raw vegetable plate

2 lbs. lean ground beef	**¼ cup catsup**
1 onion, chopped, or 2 Tbsp. dry chopped onion	**1 Tbsp. chili powder**
	1 Tbsp. brown sugar
1 (14-oz.) can pinto beans, drained and slightly mashed, optional	**1 tsp. salt**
	¼ tsp. pepper
1 (10-oz.) can chicken and rice soup	**10–12 hamburger buns**
¼ cup barbecue sauce	

Brown ground beef and onion. Drain fat. Add slightly mashed beans, soup, barbecue sauce, catsup, chili powder, brown sugar, salt, and pepper. Simmer slowly, uncovered, for about 15 minutes.

Tip: Beans are a great meat extender and blend well into meat mixture

Basic Lentils

Yield: about 2 cups

Lentils are high in protein and fiber, low in calories. They are a great meat substitute or extender. They are good in meat loaf, sloppy joe mix, tacos, enchilada fillings, salads, soups, and so on.

1 cup lentils	**½ tsp. salt**
2 cups water	

Sort lentils. Remove any foreign material and rinse. Place lentils, water, and salt in saucepan. Cover and simmer until tender, 25–35 minutes.

Tip: The older the lentils, the longer they take to cook.

Lentils

Yield: 12 to 14 servings

A satisfying main dish or side dish that keeps and freezes well.

2 cups dried lentils

5 cups water

2 Tbsp. oil

1 large onion, chopped, or
  2 Tbsp. dry chopped onion

1 green pepper, chopped

2 tsp. salt

1 (14-oz.) can diced or crushed
  tomatoes

Sort and rinse lentils. In large saucepan, combine lentils, water, oil, onion, green pepper, and salt. Bring to a boil. Reduce heat, cover, and simmer until barely tender, 20–25 minutes. Add tomatoes and simmer for 10–12 minutes.

Green Bean Casserole

Yield: 4 to 5 servings

A pleasing combination of flavors in this one-dish meal.

  Menu: Green Salad and biscuits

½–1 lb. lean ground beef

1 (10-oz.) can cream of mushroom soup

1 cup milk, or ¼ cup dry milk
  and 1 cup water

1 Tbsp. catsup

1 Tbsp. Worcestershire Sauce

2 (14-oz.) cans green beans,
  drained

3 cups mashed potatoes or dry
  potato flakes, reconstituted,
  or frozen potato nuggets

Preheat oven to 350°F. In large skillet, brown ground beef. Drain fat. Stir in soup, milk, catsup, and Worcestershire sauce. Fold in green beans. If using dry milk, whisk into mushroom soup and then stir in water. Pour into large casserole and cover top evenly with mashed potatoes or frozen potato nuggets. Bake uncovered until mixture is bubbly and potatoes are golden brown, 30–40 minutes.

» PASTA

Tip: Macaroni and spaghetti double in bulk in cooking. Noodles swell scarcely at all—only about one-fourth.

Noodles Divine

Yield: 8 servings

Menu: Glazed carrots, green salad

1 medium onion, chopped, or 2 Tbsp. dry chopped onion

2 carrots, shredded

1 Tbsp. butter

1 (10-oz.) can cream of mushroom soup

1 (4-oz.) can mushrooms, with liquid

2 cups water

dash of pepper

4 cups wide egg noodles, uncooked

1 cup chopped broccoli, fresh or frozen

2–3 cups canned chicken or tuna, with liquid

grated parmesan cheese

Sauté onion and carrot in butter in large skillet for about 3 minutes. Stir in soup, mushrooms with liquid, water, and pepper. Bring to a boil. Stir in noodles and return to boiling. Add broccoli. Reduce heat, cover, and simmer for about 15 minutes or until broccoli and noodles are tender, stirring occasionally. Add chicken or tuna to noodle mixture the last 5 minutes of cooking. Sprinkle with parmesan cheese and serve hot.

Macaroni 'n' Tomatoes

Yield: 4 to 6 servings

A quick-fix supper dish enjoyed by many.

Menu: Relish tray, hot biscuits

2 cups uncooked macaroni

1 (14-oz.) can stewed tomatoes

salt and pepper to taste

1 tsp. chili powder (to taste)

Cook and drain macaroni. Fold cooked macaroni into tomatoes. Season to taste with salt and pepper and chili powder. Heat to boiling. Simmer gently for 10–12 minutes.

Chicken Chow Mein

Yield: 5 to 6 servings

A tasty treat that is quick to make.

Menu: Fried rice, batter rolls

2 Tbsp. oil

1 large chicken breast, thinly sliced, or 2 cups canned chicken

1 medium onion, thinly sliced, or 1 Tbsp. dry chopped onion

3 stalks celery, sliced

2 carrots, thinly sliced or coarsely shredded

2 cups shredded cabbage

1 cup water

1 chicken bouillon cube or 1 tsp. chicken granules

2 Tbsp. soy or teriyaki sauce

¼ tsp. garlic powder

½ tsp. ginger

1 rounded Tbsp. cornstarch

2 pkgs. ramen noodles, cooked

Heat oil in fry pan. Add chicken and stir-fry until no longer pink. Add onion, celery, carrots, and cabbage. Stir-fry for 4–5 minutes, until tender crisp. In large measuring cup, mix water, bouillon, soy or teriyaki sauce, garlic powder, ginger, and cornstarch. Pour into chicken-vegetable mix and stir until thickened. Mix in ramen noodles. Sprinkle flavor packets from ramen noodles over all. Toss and serve immediately.

Tuna Noodle Casserole

Yield: 4 to 6 servings

2 (6-oz.) cans diced tuna, with liquid

1 (10-oz.) can cream of mushroom soup

½ soup can milk or water

1 medium onion, chopped, or 1 Tbsp. dry chopped onion

1 tsp. salt

1 cup peas or broccoli, optional

3 cups dry crinkle noodles, cooked, or 1½ cups elbow macaroni, cooked

grated cheese

Preheat oven to 350°F. Combine diced tuna, soup, milk or water, onion, and salt. Fold in peas or broccoli and drained noodles or macaroni. Pour into large casserole. Bake until hot and bubbly, 20 –25 minutes (or you can microwave on high for 8–12 minutes). Sprinkle with cheese.

Tip: Canned chicken, ham, or salmon may be used in lieu of tuna.

Mac and Cheese in a Skillet

Yield: 6 to 8 servings

Menu: Sliced tomatoes, green salad

1 Tbsp. oil

1 onion, chopped

2 cups uncooked macaroni

½ tsp. salt

dash pepper

⅛ tsp. oregano

½ tsp. dry mustard

2 cups water

2 Tbsp. flour

1 (12-oz.) can evaporated milk

1 cup shredded cheese

Heat oil in heavy skillet or electric frying pan. Add onion, uncooked macaroni, salt, pepper, oregano, and dry mustard. Cook on low, stirring occasionally, for 5–7 minutes. Add water and bring to a boil. Cover and simmer on low for 8–10 minutes or until macaroni is just tender. Sprinkle flour over macaroni and mix well. Stir in milk and cheese, adding additional milk or water if needed for desired consistency. Heat through and serve.

Salmon Macaroni Dinner

Yield: 6 to 8 servings

Menu: Creamy coleslaw

1 cup elbow macaroni

1 tsp. salt

6 cups water

1 (10-oz.) can cream of celery soup

²/₃ cup evaporated milk

1 (14-oz.) can salmon, with liquid

2 Tbsp. chopped pimiento, optional

¹/₃ cup shredded cheese

1 small onion, minced, or 1 Tbsp. dry chopped onion

Preheat oven to 350°F. In saucepan, boil macaroni in salted water until barely tender. Drain. Mix cream of celery soup and milk in large bowl. Remove and discard skin from salmon. Break salmon into pieces. Stir cooked macaroni, salmon, pimiento, cheese, and onion into soup mixture. Pour into greased baking dish. Sprinkle lightly with cheese. Bake until bubbly hot, about 25 minutes.

Tagliarini

Yield: 6 to 8 servings

Menu: Mushroom green beans, relish tray

1 lb. lean ground beef

1 onion, chopped, or 2 Tbsp. dry chopped onion

1 pkg. spaghetti sauce mix; or 1 Tbsp. sugar, ½ tsp. oregano, 1 tsp. basil

½ cup water

1 (4-oz.) can mushrooms, drained

1 (15-oz.) can corn, drained

1 (10-oz.) can cream of tomato soup

3 cups noodles, cooked and drained

Preheat oven to 350°F. Brown ground beef and onion in large pan. Drain fat. Stir in spaghetti sauce mix and water. Add mushrooms, corn, and cream of tomato soup and mix well. In a large casserole dish, alternately layer meat sauce and noodles, ending with the sauce. Cover and bake for 25–30 minutes (or microwave on high for 12–14 minutes).

Goulash

Yield: 6 servings

A great supper dish.

Menu: Baked squash, gazpacho salad

2 cups uncooked noodles

½ lb. lean ground beef

1 large onion, minced, or 2 Tbsp. dry chopped onion

4 stalks celery, diced

2 carrots, thinly sliced

1 (14-oz.) can tomatoes, cooked

½ tsp. salt

dash of pepper

1 tsp. sugar

In saucepan, cook noodles in boiling salted water until barely tender. Drain. Brown ground beef, onion, celery, and carrots. Drain fat. Add cooked noodles and tomatoes. Season with salt, pepper, and sugar. Thin with ½ cup water if needed. Cover and simmer for 10–15 minutes.

Noodles Made Easy

Yield: 3 cups cooked noodles

Need some noodles? Making your own is easy.

1 egg, beaten

½ tsp. salt

2 Tbsp. water or milk

1–1¼ cups flour

In medium bowl, whisk egg, salt, and water together; add enough flour to make medium-stiff dough. Roll very thin on floured surface and let stand for 20 minutes. Roll up loosely. Cut ¼-inch-wide slices. Unroll and let dry if desired. Drop into boiling soup or boiling salted water. Cook uncovered for about 10 minutes.

Spaghetti

A foolproof way to cook spaghetti. This recipe makes perfect spaghetti every time with no boil-overs.

3 quarts boiling water   **1 tsp. oil**

1 tsp. salt   **1 (8- to 12-oz.) pkg. spaghetti**

In large saucepan bring water, salt, and oil to a boil. Add spaghetti. Stir well and return water to boiling. Cover and remove from heat. Let stand for 12–15 minutes.

Spaghetti Sauce

Yield: 6 to 7 servings

An easy, delicious sauce for spaghetti or your favorite pasta.

Menu: Steamed broccoli, green salad, French bread

1 lb. lean ground beef

1 medium onion, chopped

1 Tbsp. minced garlic

1 pkg. spaghetti sauce mix; or 1 Tbsp. sugar, 1 tsp. oregano, 1 tsp .basil

2 (14-oz.) cans crushed tomatoes

2 (8-oz.) cans tomato sauce

1 (14-oz.) can red beans, mashed; or 1 cup cooked wheat, optional

1 (4-oz.) can mushrooms

salt and pepper to taste

Brown ground beef with onion and garlic. Drain fat. Add spaghetti sauce mix, tomatoes, tomato sauce, beans, and mushrooms and mix well. Simmer for 25–30 minutes. Serve over spaghetti.

Lentil Spaghetti Sauce

Yield: 4 to 5 servings

This wonderful sauce is high in vegetable protein.

1 onion, chopped

2 tsp. minced garlic

1 Tbsp. oil

1 (8-oz.) can tomato sauce

1 (14-oz.) can diced tomatoes

1 cup water

1 cup lentils, washed

½ tsp. oregano

1 tsp. basil

¼ tsp. salt

Sauté onion and garlic in oil. When tender, add tomato sauce, tomatoes, water, lentils, oregano, basil, and salt. Bring to a boil. Reduce heat, cover, and simmer for 25–35 minutes or until lentils are tender. Serve over hot pasta.

Quick Pasta Sauce

Yield: 4 servings

Try this when you're in a hurry.

1 (10-oz.) can cream of tomato soup

1 soup can water

1 (8-oz.) can tomato sauce

1 Tbsp. dry chopped onion

1–2 Tbsp. Italian or pizza seasoning, or 1 pkg. spaghetti sauce mix

1 cup cooked lentils, optional

ground beef, optional

In saucepan, mix tomato soup, water, tomato sauce, and onion. Add seasoning. Add lentils or cooked ground beef if desired. Bring to a boil and simmer for 8–10 minutes. Serve over your favorite pasta.

Lasagna

Yield: 12 servings

A quick-to-make-and-bake recipe that feeds a crowd.

Menu: Marinated Vegetables, French bread

1 lb. lean ground beef

1 (24-oz.) jar pasta sauce

1 (8-oz.) can tomato sauce

2 cups cottage cheese; or 1 (14-oz.) can white beans, with liquid, mashed

1 egg, slightly beaten

1 Tbsp. dry parsley

1–2 cups shredded cheese

1 (8-oz.) pkg. lasagna noodles (10 noodles)

2 cups thinly sliced zucchini, optional

Preheat oven to 350°F. In large skillet or heavy saucepan, brown ground beef and drain fat. Stir in pasta sauce and tomato sauce. In small bowl, combine cottage cheese or mashed beans, egg, parsley, and half the shredded cheese. Set aside. In 9×13 baking dish, layer one-third of sauce mixture, half the uncooked noodles (break to fit), and half the cottage cheese or bean mixture. Add a layer of thinly sliced zucchini if desired. Repeat layers, ending with sauce mixture. Cover tightly with foil. Bake until noodles are tender, 50–60 minutes. Sprinkle with remaining cheese. Let stand 10 minutes before serving. You can prepare ahead and refrigerate overnight or until needed. If so, increase baking time by 10 minutes.

Tip: If you don't have spaghetti sauce, mix 2 (14-oz.) cans crushed tomatoes, 1 tsp. oregano, 1 tsp. basil, 1 Tbsp. dry onion, 1 tsp. salt, 1 tsp. sugar.

Tip: If you don't have ground beef, add 1 cup cooked wheat kernels or bulgur wheat. Or add 1 (14-oz.) can red or pinto beans, drained and coarsely chopped.

Quick Lasagna: Cook rotini or penne pasta and use in place of lasagna noodles. Layer sauce, noodles, and cheese mix and repeat. Bake for 20–30 min at 350°F–375°F, until hot and bubbly.

Slow Cooker Lasagna

Spray a 5-quart slow cooker with cooking spray. Use Lasagna recipe (p. XX). Layer ingredients as follows: sauce, noodles (breaking to fit where necessary), sauce, noodles, cottage cheese, sauce, noodles, and remaining sauce. Top with shredded cheese. Cook on low for 4 hours or high for 2 hours. Remove cover and let stand for 15 minutes before serving.

Pizza Dough

Yield: 1 large or 2 medium pizzas

One secret of crisp homemade pizza is to prebake the crust in a very hot oven.

2½ cups flour, whole wheat or white, divided	1 cup hot water (120°F–130°F)
1 Tbsp. sugar	2 Tbsp. oil
1 tsp. instant dry yeast	Quick Pizza Sauce (see next page)
1 tsp. salt	

Preheat oven to 450°F. In bowl, mix 2 cups flour, sugar, dry yeast, and salt. Add water and oil and mix well. Add remaining flour as needed to make soft dough that is manageable to handle with oiled hands. Knead for about 5 minutes and let rest for 5 minutes. Roll or pat dough to fit lightly greased pizza pan or baking sheet. Spread sauce evenly over dough, add desired toppings, and bake for 10–12 minutes (large pizza) or 6–8 minutes (medium pizza).

Tip: To avoid soggy crust, prebake crust 3–4 minutes at 450°F. Use immediately or cool, cover and use later; crust freezes well. Top with sauce and toppings just before baking. Cheese may be added after baking if desired.

Possible toppings: Pepperoni, Canadian bacon, cooked ground beef, shrimp, grated cheese, olives, green pepper, tomatoes, pineapple tidbits, broccoli, cauliflower, onions, grated carrot, and so on.

Quick Pizza Sauce

Yield: enough sauce for 1 large pizza or 2 medium pizzas

1 Tbsp. dry spaghetti sauce
mix; or ¼ tsp. oregano, 1 tsp.
basil, 1 tsp. sugar

2 (8-oz.) cans tomato sauce

Mix dry spaghetti sauce mix (or substitutes) and tomato sauce.

A Pot Full of Beans
Is a Pot Full of Nutrition!

Beans, Beans, and More Beans

Beans are one of nature's nutritionally power-packed foods. They are one of the least processed, least chemically treated foods you can purchase today. Rich in flavor and fiber and low in fat and calories, they are an excellent choice to include in a well-balanced diet. Beans are loaded with protein, vitamins, and minerals. They are an excellent source of soluble fiber, which helps lower cholesterol and stabilize blood sugar. Because beans digest more slowly than many foods, they keep hunger at bay for longer periods—a good way to stay lean and healthy!

Beans are a good meat replacement or supplement. Try matching bean color to the foods you add them to. Many bean varieties are available, and these may be interchanged in most recipes.

If beans are new to your diet, eat small servings at first to allow your intestinal bacteria to adjust and make bean digestion more efficient. (Some people use Beano for digestion.) Eat beans regularly but as a side dish until the body adjusts. Sprouting beans slightly before cooking may help. Beans are versatile, satisfying, and inexpensive.

» Tasty Ways to Use and Enjoy Beans

- Enjoy pinto beans or refried beans in place of meat or as a meat extender in any Mexican food: burritos, casseroles, enchiladas, fajitas, tacos, taco salad, tostadas, and so on. Chili makes a delicious baked potato topper.

- Use mashed pinto or red beans as a meat extender in meat loaf.

- Red beans complement most Italian foods.

- Make a tomato and bean or lentil sauce for spaghetti or lasagna.

- White beans add satiety to a favorite noodle casserole.

- Slightly mashed white or pinto beans extend tuna or salmon.

- Beans make a hearty addition to almost any soup or stew.

- Combine beans with pasta, fish, beef, or poultry.

- Cooked beans thicken up and taste better if cooked a day ahead. They keep well in the refrigerator or the freezer.

Tips: In an emergency, mashed beans can be used as a substitute for butter, margarine, or oil in many baked goods, such as cakes and cookies. Use cooked or canned beans and mash or blend. Use the same amount of mashed beans as the fat called for in the recipe. When using in place of oil, puree beans in blender, adding just enough water to make a smooth, thick paste. Choose beans that match the color of the dough you are working with, such as black beans in chocolate cake or cookies and white beans in spice cake or oatmeal cookies. For crisper cookies, use half bean puree, half fat.

» DRY BEAN KNOW-HOW

1 cup dry beans makes about 2½ cups cooked beans

Preparing Dry Beans for Cooking

Spread beans on table or baking sheet and sort, removing shriveled or broken beans and any foreign objects. Rinse and drain beans before cooking.

Soaking and Cooking Beans

Soaking beans helps digestibility and shortens cooking time. Use twice as much water as beans and cook in the same water. Included here are several methods for soaking and cooking dry beans. If beans have been stored for a long time, they may require extra cooking time. Pressure cooking is ideal for old beans.

Overnight soak: Soak beans overnight or at least 8–10 hours.

Speed soak: Heat water and beans to boiling. Boil for 2 minutes. Remove from heat. Cover and allow beans to soak for at least 1 hour. Bring water to a boil. Reduce heat and simmer until tender, 2–3 hours.

No pre-soak: Beans can be cooked without pre-soaking, if they are not too old. Heat beans to boiling. Reduce heat and simmer until tender, 3–4 hours. Cooking time increases an hour or two over pre-soaked beans.

Easy method, no pre-soak: Cover and cook for 8 hours or overnight in a 200-degree oven. Add seasonings and cook 3–4 more hours if desired.

Slow cooker: Soak overnight in cooker. Cook on high for about 3 hours, until tender. Or if you cook on low overnight without presoaking, they're usually tender in the morning.

Pressure cooker: Pressure cookers are an ideal way to cook dry beans, especially old beans. Use the speed soak method (previous page) and cooking time is reduced to just minutes. Add 1–2 tablespoons oil to prevent foaming, which could block the pressure vent. Do not fill pan over half full. Follow pressure cooker directions for time. Old beans may take longer to cook.

Pressure cooker with no pre-soak: Pressure cooking time approximately doubles. Add 1–2 tablespoons oil to prevent foaming. Always follow manufacturer's directions for time. Pre-soaking is highly recommended.

- Baking soda produces mushy beans and depletes minerals. Although some recipes call for baking soda to speed cooking and soften beans by increasing alkalinity, use soda only if you have extremely hard water.

- **DO NOT** add salt, sugar, soy sauce, tomatoes, lemon juice, or anything acidic until beans are tender. These ingredients toughen beans and increase cooking time considerably.

- Beans thicken up and taste even better the next day. Use within 10 days. Beans freeze well and are easy to use when frozen in recipe-size packages.

Jane's Beans

Yield: about 6 cups

Discover the wonderful world of beans! This easy delicious recipe is the ideal foundation for many of our tasty bean dishes, particularly those made with pinto beans. Double the recipe and keep beans in the refrigerator or freezer so they are ready to eat.

5 cups water

2 cups pinto beans or any dried beans: red, pink, black, kidney, Great Northern, etc.

1 onion, chopped, or 2 Tbsp. dry chopped onion

1 tsp. minced garlic

1 cup mild salsa, optional

1 tsp. salt, or to taste

Mix water, beans, onion, and garlic in large heavy saucepan. Heat to boiling and boil for 2 minutes. Remove from heat. Cover and let stand for 1 hour. Bring beans to a boil, reduce heat, and simmer gently until tender, about 2–3 hours. Stir occasionally. When beans are soft, add salsa and salt. Simmer for 15–20 minutes or longer. Salsa adds a rich, wonderful flavor. Cover and store in refrigerator for up to 10 days. Beans thicken up and taste even better the next day.

Refried Beans

Yield: 2 to 3 cups

2–3 cups cooked pinto beans

1–2 tsp. chili powder

½ tsp. onion salt

½ tsp. garlic salt

salsa

Mash beans and add chili powder, onion, and garlic salt to taste. Stir in salsa to make desired consistency.

Tip: Canned beans may be used in any recipe calling for cooked dry beans. One 14-ounce can of beans yields about 2 cups.

Dehydrated Refried Beans

So quick and easy to prepare. Season as desired.

1 cup dehydrated refried beans   **seasonings of choice**

1 cup boiling water

Stir beans into boiling water. Cover and let stand for 10 minutes. Season as desired with onion and garlic salt, chili powder, and so on. Salsa adds a great flavor as well.

Layered Fiesta Dip

Yield: 18 to 20 servings

A delicious blend of flavors and almost a meal in itself,

2 (14-oz.) cans refried beans, spicy or regular, or 3–4 cups

2–4 Tbsp. salsa

1 tsp. chili powder, to taste

2–4 cups guacamole, or 3–4 large ripe avocados, peeled and mashed

2–4 Tbsp. salsa or taco sauce

½ tsp. seasoned salt, or to taste

1–2 cups sour cream

1–2 Tbsp. dry taco seasoning mix, or to taste

1 (4-oz.) can diced green chilies, drained, optional

1 cup finely shredded cheese, plus more

¼ cup chopped ripe olives

2 tomatoes, finely diced

corn tortilla chips

Mix beans, salsa, and chili powder and set aside. Combine guacamole with salsa and add seasoned salt. Set aside. Mix sour cream and taco seasoning and set aside. Layer bean mix, guacamole, sour cream mix, green chilies, shredded cheese, olives and tomatoes on a platter or in a 9×13 baking dish. Sprinkle lightly with more shredded cheese. Serve immediately with corn tortilla chips or cover and refrigerate. For best flavor, let chilled dip sit at room temperature for 30 minutes before serving.

Salsa Supreme

Yield: 8 to 12 servings

½–⅔ bunch cilantro (discard stems)

1–2 jalapeños, or to taste

½ large yellow onion, chopped

1–2 Tbsp. minced garlic

6–8 fresh tomatoes, roma or any sweet variety

½–1 fresh lime, juiced

salt to taste

garlic salt to taste

1–2 (8-oz.) cans tomato sauce, depending on how juicy tomatoes are

In a hand-crank salsa maker (available online), chop cilantro leaves. Add jalapeños and finely chop. Add and finely chop yellow onion. Add minced garlic. Add tomatoes and chop until tomatoes are well blended and slightly pureed. Add fresh lime juice, salt, and garlic salt. Add tomato sauce if needed for flavor and desired consistency. Serve with tortilla chips or any Mexican food.

Tip: You can also make this in a food processor.

Arizona Salsa

Yield: 8 to 9 cups

Freeze some for later, if there's any left.

2 (14-oz.) cans crushed tomatoes

1 (14-oz.) can diced tomatoes with green chilies; or 1 (14-oz.) can Mexican stewed tomatoes, blended

1 medium onion, chopped or finely diced

½ bunch cilantro, finely chopped, discard stems

1–2 Tbsp. fresh lemon or lime juice

1–2 Tbsp. minced garlic

1 Tbsp. menudo mix (Mexican seasoning), or ½ tsp. oregano and 1 tsp. red chili flakes or crushed red peppers

1 tsp. garlic salt, or to taste

1 Tbsp. olive oil

Mix crushed tomatoes, diced tomatoes, onion, cilantro, lemon or lime juice, garlic, menudo seasoning or substitute, garlic salt, and olive oil. Adjust seasonings to taste. Mix well and chill.

Tip: Onion and cilantro can be chopped in food processor

Favorite Chili

Yield: 10 to 12 servings

Quick, mild, and flavorful. Easy to double or triple if desired.

1 lb. lean ground beef

1 large onion, chopped, or 2
Tbsp. dry chopped onion

6 cups cooked pinto or red
beans or mix of both, or 3 (14-
oz.) cans pinto or red beans,
with liquid

1 (14-oz.) can diced tomatoes

2 cups salsa

1 cup water

1 Tbsp. chili powder

1–2 tsp. cumin

1 tsp. marjoram

2 Tbsp. sugar

2–3 tsp. salt

In large pan brown ground beef and onion. Drain fat. Add beans,
tomatoes, salsa, water, chili powder, cumin, marjoram, sugar, and
salt. Cover and simmer until flavors blend, 45–60 minutes. To thin,
add tomato juice or water as needed.

Black Bean Chili

Yield: 8 servings

You'll enjoy this tasty combination.

2 (14-oz.) cans black beans,
with liquid

1–2 (14-oz.) cans diced
tomatoes

1 medium onion, chopped, or 1
Tbsp. dry chopped onion

1 green bell pepper, chopped

1 (8-oz.) can tomato sauce

1 Tbsp. chili powder

2 tsp. cumin

dash of cayenne pepper

In large pan, mix black beans, tomatoes, onion, green pepper, tomato
sauce, chili powder, cumin, and cayenne. Bring to a boil. Reduce heat
to low. Cover and simmer for 20–25 minutes, stirring occasionally.

Chili for a Crowd

Yield: 12 to 14 servings

Chili is always better the second day.

1 lb. lean ground beef

1 large onion, diced, or 2 Tbsp. dry chopped onion

1 (14-oz.) can diced tomatoes

3 (8-oz.) cans tomato sauce

3 (14-oz.) cans pinto beans, with liquid

2 (14-oz.) cans kidney beans, with liquid

1 (4-oz.) can diced green chilies

2 cups water

2 tsp. salt

1 tsp. black pepper, to taste

2 tsp. cumin powder

2–3 Tbsp. chili powder

1 cup bulgur, optional

Brown ground beef and onion over medium heat. Drain excess fat. Add tomatoes, tomato sauce, pinto beans with liquid, kidney beans with liquid, green chilies, water, salt, pepper, cumin, and chili powder. Add bulgur if desired. Bring to a boil and simmer over low heat for 45–60 minutes, stirring every 15 minutes. Thin with water if desired. Chili freezes well. Serve with hot corn bread muffins if desired.

Fiesta Bake

Yield: 8 to 10 servings

A large recipe, so freeze some for later—cook once and eat twice!

1 lb. lean ground beef

2 tsp. minced garlic

1 onion, diced, or 2 Tbsp. dry chopped onion

1 tsp. salt

dash of pepper

1 (10-oz.) can enchilada sauce

1 (8-oz.) can tomato sauce

1 (14-oz.) can whole kernel corn, with liquid

2 (14-oz.) cans chili beans, with liquid, or 4 cups Jane's Beans (p. XX)

½ cup olives, chopped, optional

10–12 corn tortillas, torn into large pieces

1 cup finely shredded cheese

Preheat oven to 350°F. Brown ground beef, garlic, and onion. Drain fat and season with salt and pepper. Add sauces, corn, beans, and olives and mix. Place 1 cup meat mixture each in the bottom of 2 casserole dishes. Add a layer of torn tortillas. Repeat layers, ending with meat mixture. Cover and bake for 30 minutes. Sprinkle with cheese and let stand for 10 minutes before serving. Top each serving with chopped lettuce.

Tacos

Yield: 10 to 12 tacos

1 lb. lean ground beef

2 Tbsp. taco seasoning mix

1 cup water

2 cups cooked pinto, black, or refried beans

12 corn tortillas or taco shells, warmed

shredded lettuce

chopped tomato

finely chopped onion

shredded cheddar cheese

salsa or mild taco sauce, optional

In large skillet, brown ground beef and drain fat. Add taco seasoning mix, water, and beans. Heat to boiling and simmer uncovered for 10–15 minutes, stirring occasionally. Spoon about ¼ cup meat mixture into each tortilla or taco shell. Top with lettuce, tomato, onion, and cheese. If desired, add salsa or taco sauce.

Taco Sundaes

Yield: 10 to 12 servings

Serve buffet style and everyone makes their own sundae.

3–4 cups cooked rice

2 (14-oz.) cans chili

2 (14-oz.) cans pinto beans or
use meat-bean mix variation
below

2 (14-oz.) cans whole kernel
corn, drained and heated

2 cups shredded cheese

4–6 cups shredded lettuce

3–4 tomatoes, diced, or 1
(14-oz.) can diced tomatoes,
drained

1 cup ripe olives, chopped

salsa or mild taco sauce

ranch salad dressing or
Mexican ranch dressing
(ranch mixed 1:1 with salsa)

tortilla chips, crushed

Make your own sundae as follows: rice, chili and beans (or meat-bean mix), corn, cheese, lettuce, tomatoes, olives, salsa, and salad dressing. Top your sundae with crushed tortilla chips and enjoy.

Meat-Bean Mix Variation:

1 lb. lean ground beef

1–3 Tbsp. taco
seasoning, or to taste

3 (14-oz.) cans pinto beans,
drained

½ cup water

In large skillet, brown ground beef. Drain fat and stir in taco seasoning, water, and beans. Bring to a boil. Cover and simmer on low for about 15 minutes, stirring occasionally. Serve with remaining ingredients listed above.

Taco Sundae Casserole

Yield: 8 to 10 servings

Quick, easy, and satisfying.

Menu: Cornbread, fruit salad

4 cups cooked rice

2 (14-oz.) cans chili, or 1 can chili and 1 (14-oz.) can pinto beans, drained

1 (14-oz.) can whole kernel corn, drained

½ cup shredded cheese

Preheat oven to 350°F. In 9×13 pan, layer rice, chili ,and corn. Cover and bake until heated through, about 30 minutes. Sprinkle cheese on top. Serve with salsa, lettuce, tomatoes, and tortilla chips.

Corn Bread Enchiladas

Yield: 4 servings

Tasty, economical, and quick to make

corn bread

1–2 cups shredded cheese

1 onion, finely chopped

shredded lettuce

diced tomatoes

4 fried eggs, over easy

mild salsa

Quick Enchilada Sauce:

2 (8-oz.) cans tomato sauce

½ cup salsa or water

1 tsp. cumin

1 tsp. chili powder

1 tsp. sugar

Make corn bread. In saucepan mix and heat tomato sauce, salsa or water, cumin, chili powder, and sugar. Thin with water if desired to make consistency of thin gravy. Cut hot corn bread into 4- to 5-inch squares. To serve, cut each square in half horizontally and place on individual warm plates. Pour about ½ cup enchilada sauce over corn bread. Top each piece with cheese, onion, lettuce, tomatoes, fried egg, and mild salsa. Garnish with additional cheese, lettuce, and tomatoes if desired.

Enchilada Sauce

Yield: about 5 cups

An authentic enchilada sauce that enhances many dishes.

3 Tbsp. oil	¼ cup flour
1–2 Tbsp. chili powder	2 (8-oz.) cans tomato sauce
1 tsp. salt	3 cans water
2 tsp. sugar	½ cup salsa

In heavy pan, mix oil, chili powder, salt, sugar, and flour. Whisk in tomato sauce, water, and salsa. Stir constantly until sauce boils and thickens. Sauce should be thin.

Lazy-Day Enchiladas

Yield: 6 to 8 servings

This quick meal is always a hit.

2 cups chicken broth, or 2 cups water and 2 Tbsp. chicken bouillon	2 cups canned chicken, chopped (use broth)
1 (10-oz.) can green enchilada sauce	corn chips, slightly crushed
	grated cheese
3–4 Tbsp. flour	lettuce
½ cup broth or water	diced tomatoes
½ cup sour cream	chopped olives
1 (4-oz.) can diced green chilies	

Mix chicken broth, or water and bouillon, and enchilada sauce in heavy saucepan over medium heat. Thicken with flour mixed with broth or water. Stir as mixture thickens. Add sour cream, green chilies, and chicken. Heat mixture, stirring as needed. Serve over slightly crushed corn chips. Sprinkle with cheese, lettuce, tomatoes, and olives as desired. Enjoy.

Tip: The amounts of chicken, broth, and so on do not have to be exact. Cooked rice can be used in place of, or in addition to, corn chips.

Enchiladas

Yield: 12 enchiladas

Who can resist a warm plate of spicy enchiladas? Choose from two flavorful fill-ings. Beans make a flavorful and healthy meat extender

Beef Filling:

½ lb. lean ground beef

1 onion, chopped

2 cups red or pinto beans, slightly mashed

½ cup enchilada sauce

In large skillet, brown ground beef and onion. Drain fat. Add slightly mashed beans and ½ cup enchilada sauce. Simmer uncovered for 4–6 minutes.

Chicken Filling:

2 cups diced cooked chicken

1 small onion, finely chopped

1 (14-oz.) can white beans, slightly mashed

1 (4-oz.) can diced green chilies

½ cup enchilada sauce

Mix chicken, onion, slightly mashed beans, green chilies, and ½ cup enchilada sauce.

2½–3½ cups enchilada sauce, divided

12 corn tortillas

1 cup grated cheese

shredded lettuce

To assemble: Preheat oven to 375°F. Warm 2½–3½ cups enchilada sauce. Pour 1 cup sauce in 9×13 baking dish. Dip each tortilla quickly into warm sauce to soften. Divide filling among tortillas. Roll up and place seam side down in baking dish. Pour remaining sauce over enchiladas. Top with grated cheese. Bake uncovered until bubbly and hot, 20–25 minutes. Garnish with lettuce.

Easy and Quick Enchilada Variation: Prepare filling as directed. Stir in enchilada sauce. Tear 10–12 tortillas into large strips and add to mixture. Top with grated cheese and bake as directed.

Quick Enchilada Casserole

Yield: 5 to 6 servings

A good choice to serve unexpected company.

Menu: Cuban black beans, fresh vegetable plate

1 (10-oz.) can cream of chicken soup

1 soup can milk or chicken broth

1 medium onion, chopped, or 2 Tbsp. dry chopped onion

1 (4-oz.) can diced green chilies

1–2 cups diced cooked chicken, with broth, optional

10–12 corn tortillas, torn into large pieces

½ cup shredded cheese

Preheat oven to 350°F. Combine cream of chicken soup and milk or broth. Stir in onion, green chilies, chicken (optional), and tortillas. Pour into casserole dish. Cover and bake for 30–40 minutes, until hot and bubbly. Sprinkle with cheese and serve.

Chili Mac

Yield: 6 to 7 servings

Kids of all ages love this simple meal.

Menu: Vegetables and dip

1 (14-oz.) can crushed tomatoes

1 (14-oz.) can kidney beans, with liquid

1 (14-oz.) can corn, with liquid

1 onion, chopped, or 2 Tbsp. dry chopped onion

1 Tbsp. minced garlic

1 small bell pepper, diced

1 cup water

1 Tbsp. chili powder

1 tsp. cumin

1 (8-oz.) pkg. pasta spirals or macaroni

In large heavy saucepan, mix tomatoes, beans, corn, onion, garlic, bell pepper, water, and spices. Simmer over medium heat for about 20 minutes, stirring occasionally. Cook pasta in boiling water until tender. Drain and add to chili mix. Serve immediately.

Tostadas

Yield: 12 tostadas

Tostadas can be made with a variety of foods.

1 lb. lean ground beef	2 tsp. chili powder
1 onion, chopped	½ tsp. salt
1 clove garlic, minced	12 corn tortillas
1 (8-oz.) can tomato sauce	2 cups refried beans, warmed

In hot skillet, brown ground beef, onion, and garlic. Drain. Stir in tomato sauce, chili powder, and salt. Heat to boiling. Reduce heat and simmer uncovered for 10–15 minutes.

Fry tortillas in hot oiled skillet until slightly brown and crisp, about 30 seconds on each side. Drain. Keep warm in 200-degree oven.

Place a layer of refried beans on each tortilla. Divide meat mixture among tortillas. Sprinkle with cheese, lettuce, tomatoes, and any other desired toppings. Serve with salsa and sour cream if desired.

Quick Black Beans

Yield: 4 to 6 cups

A quick meal and a good source of protein.

2 (14-oz.) cans black beans, with liquid	2 Tbsp. cider vinegar
	salt to taste
2 Tbsp. dry chopped onion	3–4 cups hot cooked rice

Place beans, onion, and vinegar in large saucepan. Cover and simmer for 10–12 min. Add salt. Serve over cooked rice. Top with salsa, diced tomatoes, diced green peppers, onions, or crumbled bacon bits if desired.

Cuban Black Beans

Yield: 6 cups

Rich bean flavor. Good in enchiladas, in burritos, or as a side dish.

1 cup dry black beans	1 Tbsp. minced garlic
3 cups water	1 Tbsp. oil
1 onion, chopped, or 2 Tbsp. dry chopped onion	2 Tbsp. cider vinegar
	1 tsp. salt

Sort and wash beans. Put beans, water, onion, garlic, and oil in slow cooker or medium saucepan. Cook in slow cooker on low for 4–6 hours, or cover and simmer on the stove for 1–2 hours, until beans are almost tender. Add vinegar and salt. Simmer another 15–20 minutes, until beans are tender and liquid is thick.

Black Bean Burgers

Yield: 4 to 5 patties

These are delicious cooked on lightly oiled foil on the grill.

1 (14-oz.) can black beans, drained, or 2 cups cooked beans, drained	1 Tbsp. minced garlic
	1 tsp. Worcestershire sauce
½ onion, minced, or 1 Tbsp. dry chopped onion	1 tsp. chili powder
½ green pepper, finely diced	½ tsp. salt
1 egg	¼–½ cup fine bread crumbs

In medium bowl or food processor, put beans, onion, green pepper, egg, garlic, Worcestershire sauce, chili powder, and salt. Mix or blend until mixture is thick, chunky, and pasty—chunks help hold burgers together. If the mix has too much moisture, burgers won't hold their shape, so add bread crumbs until mixture is sticky, thick, and holds together. Cook in hot oiled skillet over medium heat until hot and crispy. Serve on toasted bun with all the fixin's.

Bean Burritos

Yield: 4 to 6 burritos

Menu: Spanish rice, green salad

2 cups refried beans, warm

4–6 flour tortillas, warm

grated cheese

onion, finely chopped

diced tomatoes

salsa

Divide warm refried beans among warm tortillas. Add grated cheese, onion, tomatoes, and salsa. Roll up and enjoy!

Pulled Pork

Yield: 18 to 20 servings

A real crowd pleaser and so easy to prepare.

1 (5- to 6-lb.) boneless pork roast

water

1 Tbsp. cumin

1 cup brown sugar

1½ cups taco sauce or salsa

1 (20-oz.) bottle root beer

Put pork roast in slow cooker and cover halfway with water. Cover slow cooker and cook on low for 12 hours. Drain and discard water. Mix cumin, brown sugar, taco sauce, and root beer. Pour over roast. Cook for 4 hours on low. Shred meat and cook for 2 more hours.

Pulled Chicken

Yield: 18 to 20 servings

A versatile delicious dish.

1 cup zesty Italian dressing

1 Tbsp. chili powder

1 Tbsp. cumin

3 cloves garlic

5 lbs. boneless, skinless chicken breasts

Combine dressing, chili powder, cumin, garlic, and chicken breasts in slow cooker. Cook on low for 4 hours. Shred meat and continue cooking for 1 additional hour.

» Rice

Chicken- or Beef-Flavored Rice Mix

Yield: 4 cups dry rice mix

A Rice-A-Roni–type mix to have ready for quick rice side dishes.

4 cups uncooked rice

¼ cup dry chicken or beef bouillon

1 tsp. salt

¼ tsp. pepper

2 tsp. dried parsley

Combine rice, bouillon, salt, pepper, and parsley in large bowl. Stir until mixed well. Put 1⅓ cups mix each into 3 (1-pint) containers. Close tightly and store in cool, dry place.

Chicken- or Beef-Flavored Rice

Yield: 4 to 6 servings

2 cups cold water

1⅓ cups Chicken- or Beef-Flavored Rice Mix (above)

1 tsp. butter or oil

Bring water to a boil. Stir in rice mix and butter or oil. Bring to a boil, cover, and reduce heat. Cook for 15–25 minutes, until liquid is absorbed and rice is tender.

Spanish Rice

Yield: 4 to 6 servings

Delicious and easy to make.

1 onion, chopped	3 cups cooked rice
1 green bell pepper, chopped	1–2 tsp. chili powder, or to taste
1 Tbsp. oil	½ tsp. sugar
1 (8-oz.) can tomato sauce	1 cup cooked ground beef, optional

In a medium skillet, sauté onion and green pepper in oil for 3 minutes. Add tomato sauce, rice, chili powder, and sugar. Add beef if desired. Cover and simmer for 10–15 minutes or until tomato sauce is absorbed. Stir occasionally and add water if desired.

Quick Spanish Rice

Yield: 4 to 5 servings

A good recipe to use on a busy day.

2–3 cups cooked rice	½ tsp. chili powder
1 cup salsa	

Simmer ingredients gently in saucepan for 8–10 minutes, until salsa is absorbed well.

Rice Pilaf

Yield: 6 to 8 servings

Pilaf is good with chicken, salmon loaf, or most any meal!

2 cups cooked rice

1 (8-oz.) can tomato sauce

1 (4-oz.) can mushrooms, with liquid

1 small onion, minced, or 1 Tbsp. dry chopped onion

½ tsp. sugar

¼ tsp. garlic salt

⅛ tsp. oregano

In heavy 2-quart pan, combine rice, tomato sauce, mushrooms with liquid, onion, sugar, garlic salt, and oregano. Cover and simmer over low heat, stirring occasionally, for 10–15 minutes.

Deep South Rice and Beans

Yield: 6 servings

Menu: Green salad and corn bread or biscuits.

2 Tbsp. oil

1 small green pepper, chopped

1 small red pepper, chopped

1 onion, finely chopped, or 1 Tbsp. dry chopped onion

1 (14-oz.) can diced tomatoes

1 (14-oz.) can kidney beans, drained

1–2 tsp. basil

½ tsp. thyme

1 tsp. salt

¼ tsp. pepper

1 tsp. Cajun spice

3 cups cooked rice, white or brown

1 cup salted peanuts, optional but good

Heat oil in a large pan. Add peppers and onion and sauté until soft, 3–4 minutes. Add tomatoes, beans, basil, thyme, salt, pepper, and Cajun spice. Cook for 2–3 minutes. Stir in cooked rice. Add peanuts just before serving if desired.

Fried Rice

Yield: 4 to 6 servings

2 Tbsp. oil

1 Tbsp. minced garlic

1 stalk celery, thinly bias-sliced

1 small onion, minced, or 1 Tbsp. dry chopped onion

1 medium carrot, shredded

1 cup sliced mushrooms, optional

4 cups cold cooked rice

½ cup whole kernel corn

2 Tbsp. soy or teriyaki sauce

2 eggs, beaten

1 tsp. soy sauce

1 cup finely diced meat, cooked, optional

Preheat oil in a wok or large skillet over medium-high heat. Add garlic, celery, onion, carrot, and mushrooms (optional). Stir-fry for 2–3 minutes, or until vegetables are tender-crisp. Add cooked rice and corn. Add meat if desired. Sprinkle with 2 tablespoons soy or teriyaki sauce and stir-fry for 2–3 minutes or until heated through. Beat eggs with 1 teaspoon soy sauce. Pour over rice mixture and stir-fry for 2–3 minutes, or until eggs are just set.

Chinese Fried Wheat

Yield: 5 to 6 servings

A chewy change from fried rice.

2 Tbsp. oil (olive oil gives savory flavor)

3 cups cooked wheat kernels

½ cup diced ham, or 1 (5-oz.) can ham, diced

1 medium onion, finely diced, or 2 Tbsp. dry chopped onion

2 Tbsp. soy sauce, or to taste

1–2 eggs

Heat oil in heavy skillet. Add wheat, ham, onion, and soy sauce. Cook and stir until mix is heated through. Hollow a center in the wheat and break in eggs. Scramble until eggs are cooked, then mix all ingredients together. Serve hot with extra soy sauce, if desired.

Baked Beans

Yield: 16 to 18 servings

Everyone loves this scrumptious recipe.

3 (14-oz.) cans pork and beans, with liquid

1 (14-oz.) can kidney beans, drained

1 large onion, chopped, or 2 Tbsp. dry chopped onion

1 green pepper, chopped (about ½ cup)

¼ cup brown sugar

¼ cup molasses

¼ cup catsup

¼ cup barbecue sauce

1 tsp. mustard

1 tsp. salt

Preheat oven to 300°F. Combine pork and beans, kidney beans, onion, green pepper, brown sugar, molasses, catsup, barbecue sauce, mustard, and salt in bean pot or casserole dish. Bake uncovered in oven for 2–3 hours (or at 375°F for 60–90 minutes). Or bake in slow cooker on low for 4–6 hours. Slow cooking is best.

Tip: Use ½ cup catsup if no barbecue sauce is available.

Tip: To cook in roaster oven, multiply the ingredients 5–6 times and cook at 325°F for 4–6 hours.

Vegetable Side Dishes

Broccoli

Yield: 5 to 6 servings

A favorite way to serve this good and good-for-you vegetable.

3–4 cups broccoli florets

⅓ cup hot water

½ tsp. salt

1 Tbsp. minced garlic (bottled)

1 Tbsp. olive oil

Place broccoli in saucepan with hot water, salt, and garlic. Bring to a boil, cover, and let steam for 3–5 minutes. Broccoli should be bright green and barely tender. Drizzle with oil and serve immediately.

Glazed Carrots

Yield: 5 to 6 servings

A flavorful addition to most any meal.

8–10 carrots, sliced, or 3–4 cups baby carrots

2 Tbsp. butter

¼ cup brown sugar

¼ tsp. salt

Steam carrots in small amount of water until crunchy tender, 5–6 minutes. Drain. Add butter, brown sugar, and salt, stirring until butter melts and sugar dissolves. Continue cooking over medium heat, turning carrots until well glazed and tender, 10–12 minutes.

Mushroom Green Beans

Yield: 6 servings

Easy to fix and serve as a juicy side dish.

2 (14-oz.) cans green beans, drained

1 (10-oz.) can cream of mushroom soup

1 (4-oz.) can mushrooms, drained

grated cheese, optional

Mix and heat beans, soup, and mushrooms over medium heat for 5–6 minutes. Sprinkle cheese on top if desired. Serve immediately.

Creamed Peas and Potatoes

Yield: 4 to 6 servings

A year-round favorite.

2–3 medium-size potatoes

1 (10-oz.) pkg. frozen petite peas

½ tsp. salt

1 Tbsp. butter

1 cup milk

1 Tbsp. cornstarch, or Cream Soup Mix (p. XX)

Peel and cube potatoes. Cook in small amount of boiling, salted water until barely tender, 10–12 minutes. Drain excess water. Add frozen peas, salt, and butter. Mix milk and cornstarch or use Cream Soup Mix. Add to vegetables and cook until thickened.

Baked Winter Squash

Yield: 6 servings

Use your microwave and squash will be ready more quickly.

**1 large piece banana squash or
any winter squash**

1–2 Tbsp. water

Preheat oven to 400°F. Peel squash, remove seeds, and cut squash into serving-size pieces. Place in a casserole dish. Add water and cover dish. Bake for 40–50 minutes, or until tender.

Tip: You can also microwave on high for 8–10 minutes or until tender. Let stand for 2 minutes.

Summer or Zucchini Squash

Yield: 4 to 6 servings

A yummy summer treat.

2 tsp. butter or oil

**3–4 young summer or zucchini
squash, sliced**

1 medium onion, diced

½ tsp. salt

⅛ tsp. pepper

Melt butter in medium saucepan. Add sliced squash and diced onion. Season with salt and pepper. Cover tightly and let steam on low heat until tender, 8–10 minutes. Squash makes it own juice, so do not add water unless squash is very dry.

Tip: You can also microwave for 5–6 minutes.

Baked Yams or Sweet Potatoes

Yield: 4 servings

Sweet and satisfying.

2 large yams or sweet potatoes

Preheat oven to 400°F. Wrap yams in foil or set on a cradle of foil to prevent dripping in the oven. Bake until tender, about 1 hour.

Tip: You can also cook this in the microwave. Prick yam with a fork. Cook on high until tender, 9–11 minutes for 1 large yam. Turn over once during cooking. Let stand for 5 minutes before serving.

Corn on the Cob

Yield: 6 servings

This corn won't have that "drowned in water" flavor.

6 ears corn, husked

Place corn in 2–3 inches of boiling water. Cover and let steam on medium-high heat for 6–8 minutes. Don't let the pot boil dry.

CHAPTER 8

Special Occasion Foods

» ## Cookies, Cakes, Desserts, and Treats

Chocolate Chip Cookies

Yield: 3 to 4 dozen

This recipe is a family favorite, especially when made with whole wheat flour.

1 cup oil or shortening	**1 cup quick oats**
1 cup brown sugar	**1 tsp. baking soda**
½ cup sugar	**½ tsp. salt**
2 eggs	**1 cup chocolate chips or raisins**
1 tsp. vanilla	**½ cup chopped nuts, optional**
2¼ cups whole wheat flour	

Preheat oven to 350°F. Cream oil or shortening, sugars, eggs, and vanilla. Add flour, oats, baking soda, and salt and mix well. Stir in chocolate chips or raisins and nuts if desired. Drop by spoonfuls onto greased baking sheet and bake until lightly browned, 8–10 minutes. Don't overbake.

Tip: When measuring flour that has been sitting for a while, fluff it up with a fork or measuring cup for more accurate measurement.

Chocolate Chip Bar Cookies: Press into lightly greased 10×15 baking sheet. Bake for 12–15 minutes.

Oatmeal Cookies

Yield: 3 to 4 dozen

1 cup packed brown sugar

½ cup sugar

1 cup shortening or oil

2 eggs

1 tsp. vanilla

1½ cups whole wheat or white flour

1 tsp. baking soda

½ tsp. baking powder

1 tsp. cinnamon

½ tsp. salt

3 cups oats

1 cup raisins

1 cup chopped nuts, optional

Preheat oven to 350°F. Cream sugars, shortening or oil, eggs, and vanilla. Stir in flour, baking soda, baking powder, cinnamon, and salt. Add oats and raisins and mix well. If desired, stir in nuts. Drop by spoonfuls onto greased baking sheet and bake until lightly browned, 10–12 minutes. Don't overbake.

Oatmeal Bar Cookies: Press dough into 10×5 baking sheet. Bake for 15–18 minutes.

Peanut Butter Cookies

Yield: 4 to 5 dozen

1 cup brown sugar

1 cup sugar

1 cup peanut butter

1 cup shortening

2 eggs

1 tsp. vanilla

2½ cups whole wheat or white flour

1 tsp. baking powder

1½ tsp. baking soda

½ tsp. salt

Preheat oven to 350°F. Cream sugars, peanut butter, shortening, eggs, and vanilla. Add flour, baking powder, baking soda, and salt. Roll into walnut-sized balls. Place on ungreased baking sheet. Flatten with back of fork dipped in sugar. Bake just until set, 8–10 minutes.

Snickerdoodles

Yield: about 5 dozen cookies

You can't stop with just one!

1 cup shortening or oil	1 tsp. baking soda
1½ cups sugar	¼ tsp. salt
2 eggs	**Topping:**
2¾ cups wheat or white flour	2 Tbsp. sugar
2 tsp. cream of tartar	2 tsp. cinnamon

Preheat oven to 400°F. Cream shortening or oil, sugar, and eggs. Add flour, cream of tartar, baking soda, and salt. Shape dough into walnut-sized balls. Mix sugar and cinnamon and roll balls in mixture. Place balls 2 inches apart on ungreased baking sheet. Cookies will puff up at first and then flatten out. Bake until lightly browned but still soft, 8–10 minutes.

Applesauce Cookies

Yield: 30 to 36 cookies

These cookies have a soft cake-like texture

1 cup sugar	1 tsp. baking soda
½ cup oil	½ tsp. salt
1 egg	½ tsp. nutmeg
1 cup applesauce	1 tsp. cinnamon
2 cups whole wheat or white flour	1 cup raisins or dates, chopped
1 cup oats	½ cup chopped nuts, optional

Preheat oven to 350°F. Mix sugar, oil, and egg until fluffy. Blend in applesauce. Add flour, oats, baking soda, salt, nutmeg, cinnamon, raisins or dates, and nuts (optional). Mix well. Drop by tablespoonfuls onto nonstick baking sheet. Bake just until set, 10–12 minutes. Don't overbake.

Molasses Crinkles

Yield: 44 to 48 cookies

Thick and chewy with crackled tops.

½ cup oil or shortening	½ tsp. salt
1 cup brown sugar	2 tsp. baking soda
1 egg	1 tsp. cinnamon
¼ cup molasses	1 tsp. ginger
1 cup white flour	1 tsp. cloves
1 cup whole wheat flour	sugar

Preheat oven to 350°F. Mix oil or shortening, brown sugar, egg, and molasses until fluffy. Add flours, salt, baking soda, cinnamon, ginger, and cloves. Mix well. Chill dough. Shape into walnut-sized balls. Dip tops in sugar. Place sugar side up, 3 inches apart, on a nonstick baking sheet. Bake just until set but not hard, 10–12 minutes.

Sugar Cookies

Yield: 4 dozen

Children love decorating these cookies for Christmas or Valentine's Day.

1 cup shortening	
1 cup sugar	½ tsp. baking soda
2 eggs	½ tsp. salt
½ tsp. vanilla	1 tsp. baking powder
3 cups white flour	½ cup sour cream

Preheat oven to 350°F. In bowl, cream shortening, sugar, eggs, and vanilla until light and fluffy. Add flour, baking soda, salt, baking powder, and sour cream and mix well. Cover bowl and chill dough for 1–1½ hours. On floured surface, roll dough ¼–½ inch thick. Cut into desired shapes. Place shapes 2 inches apart on ungreased baking sheets. Bake for 8–10 minutes. Do not overbake. Remove cookies immediately to cooling rack.

No-Roll Sugar Cookies: Shape dough into tablespoon-sized balls. Place 3 to 4 inches apart on ungreased baking sheet. Flatten with bottom of glass dipped in sugar and bake until set, 8–10 minutes. Remove cookies immediately to cooling rack.

Sugar Cookie Frosting

3 cups powdered sugar

3 Tbsp. butter

1 tsp. vanilla

1/8 tsp. salt

1–2 drops food coloring, optional

milk or water

Mix powdered sugar, butter, vanilla, salt, and food coloring. Add milk or water as needed to desired consistency. Spread on cookies.

No-Bake Chocolate Cookies

Yield: 30 to 36 cookies

Children love to make these quick cookies.

1½ cups sugar

4 Tbsp. cocoa

¼ tsp. salt

½ cup milk

½ cup butter

½ cup peanut butter

1 tsp. vanilla

3 cups oats

Mix sugar, cocoa, and salt in saucepan. Stir in milk and butter. Bring mix to a boil. Boil exactly 2 minutes, stirring constantly. Remove from heat. Quickly stir in peanut butter, vanilla, and oats. Mix well. Drop by spoonfuls on wax paper–covered baking sheet.

No-Bake Peanut Butter Cookies: Follow recipe above but omit cocoa.

Crispy Peanut Butter Treats

Yield: 24 squares

Try popcorn, cheerios, or puffed wheat for a tasty change.

1 cup sugar	**1 cup peanut butter**
1 cup light corn syrup	**6 cups crispy rice cereal; or cheerios, popcorn, etc.**

Heat sugar and corn syrup in a large heavy saucepan over medium heat. When sugar has dissolved, stir in peanut butter and mix well. Remove from heat. Add rice cereal and stir until cereal is well coated. Pour into buttered 9×13 pan and press down with buttered spatula to make bars even. Cut into squares. Store covered in cool, dry place.

Butterscotch Squares

Yield: 24 bars

These chewy bars are sometimes called "stir 'n' pour brownies."

½ cup butter or shortening	**1 Tbsp. baking powder**
1 cup brown sugar	**⅛ tsp. salt**
½ cup honey	**1 tsp. vanilla**
2 eggs, beaten	**½ cup coconut, optional**
2 cups whole wheat flour	

Preheat oven to 350°F. In saucepan, melt butter or shortening. Remove from heat and stir in brown sugar and honey. Add beaten eggs, flour, baking powder, salt, vanilla, and coconut (optional). Stir until well blended. Spread in lightly greased 9×13 pan and bake. They will rise first and are done baking just as they start to fall a bit, 14–16 minutes. Do not overbake.

Raisin Bars

Yield: 24 bars

These spicy, moist bars are popular and quick to make.

1 cup raisins

1 cup water

½ cup sugar

2 cups whole wheat or white flour

2 tsp. cinnamon

1 tsp. baking soda

½ tsp. salt

⅓ cup oil or shortening

1 egg

½ tsp. vanilla

glaze (see below)

Preheat oven to 375°F. In blender, chop raisins in water for 30–40 seconds, or until raisins are finely chopped. In large mixing bowl, combine sugar, flour, cinnamon, baking soda, and salt. Add oil or shortening, egg, vanilla and the water-raisin mix. Mix well. Pour into lightly greased 10×15 baking sheet and bake for 14–16 minutes. Remove from oven and let cool slightly while making glaze. Pour glaze onto warm cookies and spread with spatula. The thin glaze seals the cookies. Cut into bars after glaze sets.

Glaze: 2 Tbsp. hot water, 1 cup powdered sugar, ½ tsp. vanilla.

Raisin Spice Cake: Increase sugar to 1 cup. Pour batter into buttered 9×13 baking dish. Bake at 350°F for 25–30 minutes.

Pumpkin Bars

Yield: 24 to 36 bars

Fragrant and flavorful.

2 cups pumpkin

2 eggs

1 cup sugar

½ cup oil

¾ cup milk, or ¼ cup dry milk and ¾ cup water

2 cups flour, whole wheat or white

1 Tbsp. pumpkin pie spice; or 2 tsp. cinnamon, 1 sp. ginger, ¼ tsp. cloves

½ tsp. salt

1 tsp. baking soda

2 tsp. baking powder

Preheat oven to 350°F. Beat pumpkin, eggs, sugar, and oil until fluffy. Add milk or water, then flour, pumpkin pie spice or substitutes, salt, baking soda, and baking powder. If using dry milk, mix into the dry ingredients. Mix well. Bake in lightly greased 10×15 baking sheet for 14–16 minutes. Cool slightly and glaze with Raisin Bar glaze (above).

Pumpkin Cake: Pour Pumpkin Bar batter into a buttered 9×13 baking dish. Bake at 350°F for 25–30 minutes.

Banana Bars

Yield: 32 to 40 bars

A real favorite at any gathering.

1 cup sugar	1 tsp. baking powder
1/3 cup vegetable oil	1 tsp. baking soda
1 egg	1/2 tsp. salt
1 tsp. vanilla	*Glaze:*
3 bananas*, mashed (about 1 cup)	1 cup powdered sugar
	2 Tbsp. hot water
1 cup buttermilk or sour milk**	1/2 tsp. vanilla
2 cups whole wheat or white flour	

Preheat oven to 375°F. Mix together sugar, oil, egg, vanilla, and bananas. Add buttermilk or sour milk, flour, baking powder, baking soda, and salt. Mix well. Bake in a lightly greased 10×15 or 11×17 baking sheet until golden brown, 16–18 minutes. Don't overbake. Cool bars for 6–8 minutes while mixing glaze ingredients. Spread glaze evenly over top of warm bars and let cool before cutting.

1 cup mashed peaches or pears may be used in place of bananas.

**Sour milk: Put 1 tablespoon vinegar in cup, fill with milk, and let stand for 5 minutes.*

Banana Cake: Pour Banana Bar batter into a lightly greased 9×13 baking dish. Bake at 350°F for 25–30 minutes.

Texas Sheet Cake Brownies

Yield: 32 pieces

An easy version of an old favorite.

2 cups flour	1 cup water
1½–2 cups sugar	1 cup oil
¼ cup cocoa	½ cup sour cream or buttermilk
1 tsp. baking soda	2 eggs
½ tsp. salt	1 tsp. vanilla

Frosting:

4 Tbsp. butter	1 tsp. vanilla
2 Tbsp. cocoa	2–3 cups powdered sugar
¼ cup hot water	

Preheat oven to 375°F. Mix flour, sugar, cocoa, baking soda, and salt. Stir in water, oil, sour cream or buttermilk, eggs, and vanilla. Beat until well mixed. Pour into greased 10×15 pan and bake for 18–20 minutes. Cool for 8–10 minutes before frosting.

For the frosting, melt butter in microwave. Stir in cocoa. Add hot water, vanilla, and powdered sugar. Mix well. Spread evenly over warm cake.

Gingerbread

Yield: 12 pieces

Makes a hit with family and friends.

½ cup oil	½ tsp. salt
1 cup sugar	1 tsp. baking soda
1 egg	1 tsp. ginger
½ cup light molasses	1 tsp. cinnamon
2 cups flour, whole wheat or white	½ tsp. cloves
	1 cup hot water

Preheat oven to 350°F. Mix oil, sugar, egg, and molasses. Stir in flour, salt, baking soda, ginger, cinnamon, cloves, and hot water. Mix well. Pour into 9×13 baking pan coated with nonstick spray. Bake until toothpick inserted in center comes out clean, 25–30 minutes. Serve with sauce (below) or whipped cream.

Gingerbread Sauce

Yield: about 1½ cups

1½ cups water	2 Tbsp. cornstarch
½ cup brown sugar	1 tsp. vanilla
2 Tbsp. butter	

Combine ingredients and cook over medium heat until mixture comes to a boil and thickens, stirring constantly. Spoon warm sauce over individual servings.

Oatmeal Cake

Yield: 15 pieces

Moist and delicious.

1½ cups boiling water

⅓ cup butter or margarine

1 cup oats

1 cup sugar

1 cup brown sugar, packed

1 egg

1 tsp. vanilla

2 cups flour, whole wheat or white

1 tsp. baking soda

½ tsp. salt

1 tsp. cinnamon

¼ tsp. nutmeg

Preheat oven to 350°F. Stir butter and oats into boiling water and set aside. Mix sugars, egg, and vanilla until creamy. Add oatmeal mixture, flour, baking soda, salt, cinnamon, and nutmeg and mix well. Pour into lightly greased 9×13 baking dish and bake for 30–35 minutes. This is delicious topped with Broiled Coconut Topping (see below).

Broiled Coconut Topping

A mouthwatering topping.

1 cup brown sugar

¼ cup water

¼ cup butter

1 tsp. vanilla

½ cup shredded coconut

1 cup oats

½ cup chopped pecans

Mix brown sugar, water, and butter in small saucepan. Bring to a boil, stirring constantly. Remove from heat and stir in vanilla, coconut, oats, and pecans. Spread over top of cake. Place cake under broiler for 1–2 minutes, until mixture bubbles and turns golden brown. Watch carefully since frosting burns easily.

Applesauce Cake

Yield: 15 to 18 pieces

A delicious cake made without eggs. The variations are flavorful too.

½ cup oil

1 cup sugar or honey

1 cup applesauce*

2 cups flour, whole wheat or white

½ tsp. salt

1 tsp. baking soda

1 tsp. baking powder

1 tsp. cinnamon

½ tsp. cloves

½ tsp. nutmeg

½ cup raisins

1 cup chopped pecans, optional

Preheat oven to 350°F. Combine oil, sugar or honey, applesauce, flour, salt, baking soda, baking powder, cinnamon, cloves, and nutmeg in bowl. Mix on medium speed for 3–4 minutes. Stir in raisins and pecans if desired. Pour into a lightly greased 9×13 pan. Bake until cake springs back when touched in center, 24–28 minutes. Cool slightly. Spread with Broiled Coconut Topping if desired (p. XX).

1 cup pureed peaches, pears, or apricots may be used instead.

Zucchini or Apple Cake: Replace applesauce with 2 cups shredded zucchini or 2 cups chopped apples.

Scrumptious Fruitcake

Yield: 30 to 35 pieces

This prize-winning cake is perfect to serve at a large family or social gathering.

3–4 cups canned fruit, with juice

1½ cups sugar

½ cup oil

4 cups whole wheat or white flour

4 tsp. baking soda

1 tsp. salt

1 tsp. cloves

1 tsp. nutmeg

1 Tbsp. cinnamon

1 cup raisins, nuts, or coconut

Preheat oven to 350°F. Blend fruit with juice in food processor or blender, or use a potato masher—it need not be a fine puree. Add sugar and oil to fruit and mix together. Add flour, baking soda, salt, cloves, nutmeg, and cinnamon. Mix well for 3–4 minutes. Stir in raisins, nuts, or coconut. Pour batter into a lightly greased 11×17 baking sheet or two 9×13 baking pans and bake for 28–30 minutes. Cake is rich and can be eaten plain, with a glaze, or with Caramel Frosting (below).

Caramel Frosting

Adds a gourmet touch to cinnamon rolls and most any cake.

⅓ cup water

⅓ cup butter

⅔ cup brown sugar

1 tsp. vanilla

pinch of salt

2–3 cups powdered sugar

Heat water, butter, and brown sugar until bubbly. Let cool. Add vanilla and salt. Stir in powdered sugar until frosting reaches desired consistency and is smooth, creamy, and easy to spread.

Lemon Bundt Cake

Yield: 16 to 18 servings

This delicious moist cake is a birthday tradition for many.

1 lemon or yellow cake mix

1 (3-oz.) pkg. instant lemon pudding

1 cup water

½ cup oil

4 eggs

Glaze:

1–2 cups powdered sugar

4 Tbsp. fresh lemon juice

4 Tbsp. orange juice

Preheat oven to 350°F. Place cake mix, pudding, water, oil, and eggs in mixer bowl. Beat for 5–7 minutes. Pour into a greased and floured bundt pan. Place a shallow pan of water on the bottom oven rack under cake. Bake for 45 minutes. While cake is baking, combine powdered sugar, lemon juice, and orange juice. Remove cake from oven and immediately remove from pan. Place on a wire cooling rack and place the rack over a large plate. Slowly pour glaze over cake, repeating several times. Serve when cool.

Chocolate Cake

Yield: 15 pieces

An easy, delicious cake.

3 cups flour	2 cups water
2 cups sugar	¾ cup oil
⅓ cup cocoa	2 Tbsp. vinegar
1 tsp. salt	2 tsp. vanilla
2 tsp. baking soda	

Preheat oven to 350°F. Mix flour, sugar, cocoa, salt, and baking soda. Add water, oil, vinegar, and vanilla. Mix until smooth. Pour into greased 9×13 cake pan and bake for 35–40 minutes.

Chocolate Frosting

Yield: enough for a 9x13 cake or 24 cupcakes

2 Tbsp. butter	3 cups powdered sugar
1 tsp. vanilla	¼ cup cocoa
⅓ cup hot milk or water	⅛ tsp. salt

Put butter and vanilla into hot milk or water and stir until butter melts. Gradually add powdered sugar, cocoa, and salt and beat until smooth.

White Cake

Yield: 15 pieces

This makes an elegant white cake. Top with strawberry sauce (see below) for a luscious shortcake.

½ cup shortening or
  vegetable oil

1 cup sugar

2 eggs

1 tsp. vanilla

2 cups white flour

½ tsp. salt

1 Tbsp. baking powder

1 cup milk, or ¼ cup dry milk
  and 1 cup water

2 eggs

Preheat oven to 350°F. Cream shortening or oil, sugar, eggs, and vanilla. Mix in flour, salt, and baking powder. If using dry milk, mix into the dry ingredients. Add milk or water and beat for 2 minutes. Pour into greased and floured 9×13 pan or large baking sheet and bake for 20–25 minutes.

Strawberry or Raspberry Sauce

Yield: 5 to 6 cups

A yummy topping for 3-2-1 Cake (p. XX), ice cream, and so on.

1 (3-oz.) pkg. strawberry
  or raspberry gelatin

1 cup sugar

¼ cup cornstarch

½ tsp. salt

3 cups water

2 Tbsp. lemon juice or
  ½ tsp. citric acid

2–4 cups sliced or crushed
  strawberries or raspberries

Mix gelatin, sugar, cornstarch, and salt in medium pan. Stir in water and lemon juice or citric acid. Cook on medium heat until mixture comes to a full rolling boil, stirring constantly. Remove from heat and let cool. Add berries. Cover and chill. Sauce thickens as it cools. Thin with water if desired.

Buttercream Frosting

Yield: enough for a 9x13 cake or 24 cupcakes

**3–3½ cups powdered sugar
  (1 lb.)**

½ cup butter or shortening

4 Tbsp. milk or water

½ tsp. vanilla

½ tsp. lemon extract

⅛ tsp. salt

Combine powdered sugar, butter or shortening, milk or water, vanilla, lemon extract, and salt. Beat for about 3 minutes at medium speed, until smooth and creamy.

3-2-1 Cake

Yield: 1 little cake

Amazing individual cakes ready to eat in one minute. Insert a candle and sing "Happy Birthday."

Cake Mix:

1 angel food cake mix

1 cake mix, any flavor (white, carrot, red velvet, spice, etc.)

For each serving:

3 Tbsp. cake mix combo

2 Tbsp. water

Combine the two cake mixes in a sealable plastic bag and mix well. Mix 3 tablespoons cake mix and water in small microwave-safe container. Microwave on high for 1 minute. Top cake with fruit sauce and a dollop of whipped topping or ice cream

Tip: Store cake mixture in sealed plastic bag or closed container in pantry; no need to refrigerate. Write recipe on bag or container.

Cherry or Blueberry Cobbler

Yield: 12 to 15 servings

An easy and succulent dessert.

1 (20-oz.) can cherry, apple, or blueberry pie filling

1 (20-oz.) can crushed pineapple, with liquid

1 Tbsp. lemon juice

1 white, lemon, or yellow cake mix

½ cup butter or margarine

½ cup chopped nuts, optional

Preheat oven to 350°F. Mix pie filling, pineapple, and lemon juice. Pour into a 9×13 baking dish. Sprinkle cake mix evenly over top of fruit. Slice butter evenly over top of cake mix. Sprinkle with chopped nuts if desired. Bake uncovered until done, 50–60 minutes. Serve with whipped cream or ice cream.

Slow Cooker Cobbler: Follow above recipe, but combine cake mix and butter or oil. Mixture will be crumbly. Sprinkle cake mixture over pie filling and pineapple. Add nuts if desired. Bake on low for 2–3 hours.

Fruit Cobbler

Yield: 10 to 12 servings

This cobbler makes its own crust while baking—like magic!

3 Tbsp. butter

1 cup flour

½ cup sugar

2 tsp. baking powder

½ tsp. salt

¾ cup milk, or ¼ cup dry milk and ¾ cup water

1 tsp. vanilla

4 cups sliced canned fruit and juice (peaches, pears, apricots, etc.)

Preheat oven to 350°F. While oven preheats, melt butter in 8×12 baking dish or 1½-quart casserole dish in the oven. Remove from oven. In bowl, mix flour, sugar, baking powder, and salt. (If using dry milk, mix into dry ingredients.) Add milk or water and vanilla. Mix well. Pour batter over melted butter. Spread fruit and juice evenly over batter. Do not stir. Bake uncovered until golden, 25–35 minutes.

New England Pie

Yield: 1 (9-inch) pie

An unbelievably easy, scrumptious pie.

¾ cup sugar

½ cup flour

¼ tsp. cinnamon

¼ tsp. nutmeg

1 tsp. baking powder

¼ tsp. salt

1 egg, slightly beaten

1 tsp. vanilla

1½ cups thinly sliced apples (2–3 apples) or dried apples, soaked

1 cup chopped nuts

Preheat oven to 325°F. Mix sugar, flour, cinnamon, nutmeg, baking powder, and salt by hand. Add egg and vanilla and mix well. Stir in apples and nuts. Pack mixture into a buttered 9-inch pie pan and bake until toothpick inserted in center comes out clean, 35–45 minutes. Serve with ice cream or whipped cream.

Easy Pie Crust

Yield: 2 (9-inch) pie shells

2 cups flour

3 Tbsp. sugar

1 tsp. salt

1 cup shortening

¼ cup cold water

Preheat oven to 400°F. Mix flour, sugar, and salt. Cut shortening into flour and mix until size of peas, using mixer, knives, or pastry blender. Sprinkle with water, one tablespoon at a time, mixing lightly with a fork until all flour is moistened. Press firmly together and form pastry into 2 balls to make 2 pie shells. Roll out dough on well-floured surface, using enough flour so pastry doesn't stick. Place dough in pie pan, crimp edges of crust, and bake for 10–12 minutes. Dough may be stored in a sealable plastic bag in refrigerator. Remove excess air before sealing.

Pumpkin Pie

Yield: 1 (9-inch) pie

An autumn favorite. Delicious just as a pie, as a pudding, or in Pumpkin Pie Squares (see next page).

2 eggs, slightly beaten	**½ tsp. ginger**
1 (14-oz.) can pumpkin	**¼ tsp. cloves**
¾ cup sugar	**1 (12-oz.) can evaporated milk**
½ tsp. salt	**1 (9-inch) pie crust**
1 tsp. cinnamon	

Preheat oven to 425°F. Mix eggs, pumpkin, sugar, salt, cinnamon, ginger, and cloves. Stir in evaporated milk and mix well. Pour mixture into 9-inch pie crust. Bake for 15 minutes in 425-degree oven and then reduce temperature to 350°F. Bake an additional 35–40 minutes or until knife inserted into center of pie comes out clean. Let cool.

Pumpkin Custard: Bake mixture without a crust until set. Watch carefully.

Pumpkin Pie Squares

Yield: 24 squares

An easy to make and serve recipe using the Pumpkin Pie recipe (previous page).

Pumpkin Pie filling (see previous page)

Crust:

1 cup whole wheat flour

½ cup oats

¼ cup brown sugar

¹/₃ cup butter or margarine

Preheat oven to 350°F. Combine flour, oats, brown sugar, and butter. Mix until crumbly. Press into ungreased 9×13 pan and bake for 15 minutes. Pour filling into baked crust and bake for 20 minutes. Remove from oven and add topping (see below). Return to oven. Bake for 15–20 more minutes or until filling is set. Cool in pan. Cut in squares. Top each square with a dollop of whipped cream or Dream Whip and a pecan half.

Topping:

¼ cup brown sugar

2 Tbsp. butter

½ cup chopped pecans

Combine brown sugar, butter, and pecans.

Applesauce Deluxe

Yield: 6 to 8 servings

Children as well as adults enjoy this healthy fruit combo.

2 (14-oz.) cans applesauce
1 cup crushed pineapple

peach yogurt, optional

Mix applesauce and pineapple. Chill. Top each serving with a dollop of yogurt if desired. Keeps well in refrigerator.

Quick Rice Pudding

Yield: 6 to 8 servings

Takes just minutes!

1 (5-oz.) pkg. vanilla pudding mix
3 cups milk, or ¾ cup dry milk and 3 cups water

1½ cups cooked rice
½ cup raisins

Stir pudding mix into 3 cups milk in medium saucepan, or mix dry milk and pudding mix, then whisk in water. Cook on medium heat until mixture comes to a full boil, 5–7 minutes, stirring constantly. Remove from heat and stir in rice and raisins. Pudding thickens as it cools. Cover and chill.

Popcorn Balls

Yield: 15 to 18 small balls

Always a favorite.

½ cup butter

1 (16-oz.) pkg. mini
  marshmallows

¼ tsp. salt

½ tsp. vanilla

few drops of green food
  coloring

6 quarts popped corn

Melt butter over low heat. Stir in marshmallows until all are melted. Add salt, vanilla, and food coloring. Remove unpopped kernels from popped corn by shaking the popped corn in a large bowl—unpopped kernels will fall to the bottom. Carefully transfer popped corn into another bowl, and pour syrup over popcorn. Mix well and shape into small balls. Cool on waxed paper.

Karamel Corn

Yield: 20 servings

Fun to serve to company on Sunday evenings.

2 cups brown sugar

½ cup butter

½ cup light corn syrup

2 Tbsp. water

1 tsp. vanilla

5–6 quarts popped corn, or
  puffed wheat and 1 cup salted
  peanuts

Heat all ingredients except vanilla and corn in a heavy saucepan. Bring to a boil and cook for 3–4 minutes, stirring constantly. Add vanilla. Remove any unpopped kernels from popcorn. Pour syrup over popcorn and mix well. Cool and break into pieces.

Blender Ice Cream

Yield: 4 servings

Satisfies your sweet tooth.

2 cups milk or yogurt

1 tsp. lemon juice

1 large banana, frozen

2 cups frozen fruit (berries, peaches, etc.)

2–3 Tbsp. honey, sugar, or agave (to taste)

½ tsp. vanilla

Put milk or yogurt, lemon juice, banana, fruit, honey (or substitute), and vanilla in blender. Pulse, then blend, until mixture is thick and smooth.

Tip: Use fresh fruit and add ice cubes to desired consistency.

Jerky

Yield: 36 to 48 strips

A tried and proven recipe.

2 lbs. beef, venison, or elk; or 2 lbs. lean ground meat

¼ cup soy sauce

1 Tbsp. fresh lemon juice or Worcestershire sauce

¼ tsp. garlic powder

¼ tsp. fresh pepper

¹/₈ tsp. ginger

¼ tsp. salt

1 tsp. liquid smoke

Soak wild meat 15 minutes in salty water. Slice slightly frozen meat ⅛ to ¼ inch thick. Mix soy sauce, lemon juice or Worcestershire sauce, garlic powder, pepper, ginger, salt, and liquid smoke. Pour this marinade over meat or mix into ground meat. Jerky can be dried immediately, but for best flavor, cover and marinate for 2–8 hours in refrigerator. If using ground meat, form meat into thin patties of desired size. Dry slices or patties in dehydrator for 4–6 hours, or until dry. Stores best in freezer.

» Lite Jams

Delicious jams that can easily be adapted to almost any desired fruit combination. Enjoy the natural fruit flavors

Strawberry Rhubarb Jam

Yield: 5-6 cups

5 cups cut rhubarb (1-inch pieces)

3–4 cups sugar, or to taste

½ cup water

1 cup mashed strawberries, optional

1 (3-oz.) pkg. strawberry gelatin

Combine rhubarb, sugar, and water in heavy saucepan. Add strawberries if desired. Bring to a boil and simmer for 15 minutes, uncovered, stirring occasionally. Stir in gelatin, mixing well. Remove from heat. Ladle jam into sterilized jars or freezer containers. Refrigerate, freeze, or seal.

Freezer Berry Jam

Yield: 5 to 6 cups

Makes delicious strawberry or raspberry jam.

5 cups stemmed and crushed berries

½ cup light corn syrup

2–3 cups sugar, or to taste

⅓ cup Ultra Gel*

Mix berries and corn syrup. Separately, mix sugar and Ultra Gel. Stir sugar mixture into fruit, mixing well. Allow 10–15 minutes for mixture to fully thicken. Pour into containers and refrigerate or freeze.

*Ultra Gel is a "modified food starch," which can be used to thicken hot or cold foods without cooking and is ideal for frozen jams. Available in many supermarkets, health food stores, and so on.

FEEDING A CROWD

Choose your favorite recipes and double or triple ingredients, depending on amount needed. Wheat, beans, macaroni, and spaghetti double in volume when cooked. Rice will triple in volume. Remember that soup and bread recipes easily adjust to feeding a large group. Therefore, any of these foods will feed a crowd simply and inexpensively. The following recipes are found in this book. Check the index for page numbers.

» Breakfast for a Crowd

Cracked Wheat Cereal

Millet Cereal

Cornmeal Mush

Rice 'n' Cinnamon

Pancake Master Mix

Pancake Syrup

Lunch or Dinner for a Crowd

Creamy Taco Soup

Hamburger Soup

Black Bean Soup

Goulash

Fiesta Bake

Quick Enchilada Casserole

Chicken and Wild Rice Soup

Chicken Noodle Soup

Split Pea Soup

Minestrone Soup

Nine-Bean Soup

Lentil Rice Stew

Lentil Vegetable Soup

Barley, Rice, and Lentil Soup	Chili	Jane's Beans
Potato Soup	Savory Baked Beans	Spaghetti
Ham and White Bean Soup	Cheesy Potatoes	Noodles Divine
Beef Stew	Taco Sundaes	Tuna Noodle Casserole
Stew in Five Minutes	Hawaiian Haystacks	Creamed Tuna or Chicken

---

Pancake Syrup

Yield: serves 50

12 cups sugar	8 cups water
1/3 cup cornstarch	2 Tbsp. maple flavoring
1/4 tsp. salt	

Mix sugar, cornstarch, and salt in a large saucepan. Add water and mix well. Bring to a boil, reduce heat, and simmer for about 10 minutes, or until thickened. Remove from heat and stir in flavoring. Syrup will thicken further upon cooling. Thin with water if desired.

Rice 'n' Cinnamon

Yield: serves 25

7 cups white rice	1/3 cup oil
14 cups water	1 cup sugar mixed with
2 Tbsp. salt	1 Tbsp. cinnamon

Cook rice in boiling salted water. Add oil and mix well. Serve hot with cinnamon and sugar sprinkled on top.

CHAPTER 9

Baby Food Made Easy

Homemade baby food is quick and easy to make. It can save hundreds of dollars and is more nutritious for babies. It takes about a one hour block of time every two to three weeks to prepare an ample food supply for your infant. Make cereal, pureed vegetables, fruits, beans, and meat. Use as needed. Freeze the extra in ice cube trays until set. Place frozen cubes in freezer bag. Label the bag and freeze for up to three months. Be creative in your food combinations and baby will enjoy it and thrive.

Pureed foods are ideal for people who cannot eat whole foods and can be prepared much the same as for baby food.

» Introducing Solid Foods

Solid foods may be introduced into a baby's diet around six months. The American Academy of Pediatrics states, "By tradition, single-grain cereals are usually introduced first. However, there is no medical evidence that introducing solid foods in any particular order has an advantage for your baby."

Additionally: "Once your baby learns to eat one food, gradually give him other foods. Give your baby one new food at a time, and wait at least 2 to 3 days before starting another. After each new food, watch for any allergic reactions such as diarrhea, rash, or vomiting. If any of these occur, stop using the new food and consult with your child's doctor" (American Academy of Pediatrics, "Switching to Solid Foods").

Cereals

Oatmeal Cereal

¼ cup quick or   **¾ cup water**
  old-fashioned oats

Stir oats into water. Bring to a boil and cook until thickened, about 5–7 minutes. Cool.

Tip: For finer texture, make oat flour in blender. Bring ½ cup water to boil, stir in 2–4 tablespoons oat flour, and cook until desired consistency. Cool. Add pureed fruit if desired.

Tip: To make in microwave, cook at 90 percent power for about 2 minutes. Cool. Add fruit if desired, such as applesauce or mashed banana or any pureed fruit.

Rice Cereal

½ cup cooked rice, brown or   **3–4 Tbsp. water**
  white

Put rice in blender and puree, adding water to desired consistency. If desired, add applesauce, mashed banana, and so on.

» Pureed Vegetables & Fruit

Fresh, frozen, or canned.

Follow directions below to prepare, puree, and freeze:

To cook fresh or frozen vegetables such as carrots, broccoli, green beans, or summer squash, place in pan with 1–2 inches water. Cook until fork tender. To optimize nutrition, add the cooking liquid as needed when pureeing vegetables. Cooked fresh green beans may need to be strained through a fine mesh strainer to remove strings.

To prepare cooked vegetables: Put vegetables in blender. Add cooking liquid or water and puree to desired consistency. Freeze puree in ice cube trays until set. Place frozen vegetable cubes in freezer bags. Label the bags and freeze until needed.

Pureed Carrots

3 cups carrots, cooked　　　　**⅓ cup water**

See above for directions.

Pureed Green Beans, Broccoli, or Peas

1 cup green beans, broccoli, or peas; cooked　　　　**2–4 Tbsp. water**

See above for directions.

Pureed Spinach

1 (10-oz.) frozen spinach, cooked **1–3 Tbsp. water, if needed**

See previous page for directions.

Pureed Summer Squash

1½ cups squash, cooked **2–4 Tbsp. water**

See previous page for directions.

Pureed Banana Squash or Butternut Squash

¼ banana squash or 1 medium butternut squash **water**

Cut squash into pieces. Remove seeds if needed. Place into micro-wave-safe dish and add 1–2 inches water. Cover and microwave until fork tender, 8–10 minutes. Let cool. Remove peel. Place squash in blender, add cooking water as needed, and puree to desired consistency.

Pureed Sweet Potatoes or Yams

1 sweet potato or yam, cooked **⅓–½ cup water**

Preheat oven to 400°F. Scrub outside of sweet potato or yam. Pierce with fork and wrap in foil. Place on foil- or parchment paper–lined baking sheet and bake for 45–60 minutes. Remove from oven and cool before removing skin. Place in blender and puree, adding water as needed for desired consistency.

Pureed Fruit

2 cups fresh or frozen fruit,   **water as needed**
   peeled (peaches, pears,
   bananas, etc.)

Place fruit in blender and puree. Add water if needed.

Pureed Canned Fruit

canned fruit (apricots, peaches,   **water or juice as needed**
   pears, etc.)

Use only fruit canned in juice, not syrup. Drain juice and set aside. Put fruit in blender and puree to desired consistency. Add water or juice if needed. Freeze in ice cube trays until set. Place frozen cubes in freezer bag. Label and date the bag. Store in freezer.

Applesauce

Yield: 2 to 3 cups

4–6 apples

Cut apples into fourths. Peel and core. Place in a saucepan. Barely cover apples with water and boil until fork tender. Remove from heat and cool slightly. Put apples in blender and blend until smooth. Add cooking water as needed to desired consistency.

Tip: Unsweetened applesauce is a good fruit to mix in cereal, canned beans, or cooked chicken breasts.

» Cooked Beans

The current recommendation for when to introduce cooked dried beans, lentils, and legumes into a baby's diet is eight to ten months. These foods are high protein, and babies may not have the ability to digest them until this age. Legumes, beans, and lentils cause few allergic reactions in babies. Discuss any feeding issues with your child's pediatrician.

Pureed Pinto, White, Kidney, or Black Beans

1 (14-oz.) can beans, rinsed and drained, or 2 cups cooked beans

Puree beans in blender to desired consistency, adding water as needed.

Mixed Vegetable and Bean Puree

¼ cup cooked beans (pinto, white, kidney, black beans, etc.)

¼ cup tender cooked greens (spinach, kale, green beans, etc.)

1–3 Tbsp. water

Puree beans and greens, adding water to desired consistency. Freeze in meal-size portions until needed.

Pureed Meat

Meat is not recommended until a baby is at least ten months old.

Pureed Chicken or Beef

1 cup cooked and cubed chicken or beef

¼–⅓ cup water

Place chicken and water in blender and puree to desired consistency. Freeze in ice cube trays until set. Place frozen cubes in ziplock bags. Label and date the bags. Freeze until needed.

Tip: As babies get older, around 10 months, regular healthy table food can be ground up in a baby food grinder and served for meals. Babies can sit at the table or high chair and enjoy the meal with everyone else. Baby food grinders are readily available online or in the baby section of some retail stores.

Pureed Meat or Beans and Vegetables

2–3 cubes frozen pureed vegetables (p. 218)

1 cube frozen pureed cooked meat (see above) or frozen pureed beans (previous page)

Let cubes thaw in refrigerator. Warm or thaw in microwave. Mix vegetables and meat or beans and serve.

Emergency Infant Formulas

These baby formula recipes are intended to be used *only* in an emergency situation! Vitamins A, D, and C should be provided from the time of birth in the milk or by supplement. If the infant does not receive adequate amounts of these vitamins, he will develop deficiency symptoms in one to three months, depending on his body reserves. Store infant vitamin drops and keep them rotated in case they are needed. The following recipes were adapted from Kay Franz's *Maintaining Nutritional Accuracy*, with permission from the author.

Emergency Evaporated Milk Formula

1 (12-oz.) can evaporated milk

2 Tbsp. sugar or corn syrup

boiled water, cooled

Mix evaporated milk and sugar or syrup. Add boiled water to equal 1 quart (4 cups).

Emergency Nonfat Dry Milk Baby Formula

¾ cup non-instant nonfat dry milk or 1 cup plus 2 Tbsp. instant nonfat dry milk

about 4 cups boiled water (cooled), divided

2 Tbsp. sugar or light corn syrup

3 Tbsp. vegetable oil

Whisk dry milk and 3 cups of the boiled water together. Mix thoroughly. Add sugar or corn syrup and oil. Mix well. Add remaining boiled water to equal 4 cups (1 quart).

Emergency Baby Formula

3 Tbsp. non-instant dry milk

1 cup boiled water, cooled

1 Tbsp. oil

1½ tsp. sugar or corn syrup

Whisk dry milk and water together. Mix thoroughly. Add oil and sugar or corn syrup. Mix well. Place in sterilized baby bottles. If a baby bottle is not available, milk can be spoon-fed to an infant.

Emergency Baby Food

This can be fed to infants under 6 months IF adequate milk is not available, but it must be pureed to a very fine texture. The grain–legume combination will provide needed calories, protein, and iron.

water

¾ cup cereal grains (oatmeal is a common one)

¼ cup cooked beans (pinto, red, or navy) or legumes (split peas, lentils)

Add water and ingredients to saucepan and boil until soft. Puree until smooth, adding water to desired consistency.

CHAPTER 10

Emergency Cooking Solutions

» To Reconstitute Dry Milk

Amount	Non-Instant	Instant	Water
1 quart	¾ cup	1⅓ cups	2 scant cups
1 pint	⅓ cup	⅔ cup	2 scant cups
1 cup	3 Tbsp.	⅓ cup	1 scant cup
½ cup	2 Tbsp.	3 Tbsp.	½ cup
¼ cup	1 Tbsp.	1½ Tbsp.	¼ cup

» To Use Dry Milk in Recipes

- In recipes for baked goods that call for milk, stir the dry milk into the other dry ingredients. Use water in place of milk called for in the recipe. Most recipes in this book use non-instant dry milk.

- In reconstituting any canned creamed soup concentrate—such as tomato, chicken, mushroom, and so on—whisk dry milk into soup concentrate and then stir in a can of water.

- To make extra-creamy home-made cream soup, mix dry milk with dry ingredients. Use regular milk in place of the water.

- For cooked cereals, add ¼–½ cup dry milk to each cup of cereal before cooking.

Buttermilk or Sour Milk

Yield: 1 cup

¼ cup dry milk　　　　　　　　**1 scant cup water**
1 Tbsp. vinegar or lemon juice

Mix dry milk into dry ingredients in chosen recipe. Mix venegar (or lemon juice) and water and add as liquid.

Option 2: Put vinegar or lemon juice in cup and add water to equal 1 cup. Mix in dry milk using blender or wire whisk. Let mix sit undisturbed for 5–10 minutes. Amount of liquid in recipe may need to be reduced slightly.

Evaporated Milk

Yield: amount equal to 1 can evaporated milk

⅔ cup dry milk　　　　　　　　**1 cup water**

Mix dry milk and water using whisk or blender until smooth.

Sweetened Condensed Milk

Yield: amount equal to 1 can sweetened condensed milk

1 cup sugar　　　　　　　　**½ cup very hot water**
1 cup dry milk　　　　　　　　**2 Tbsp. butter**

Mix sugar and dry milk. Whisk in hot water and butter and mix until smooth.

Tip: You can also place all ingredients in blender and blend until smooth.

Whipped Topping

1 cup dry milk
1/3 cup ice water
1 Tbsp. lemon juice

1 tsp. vanilla
3 Tbsp. sugar

Chill bowl and beater. Beat milk and ice water together until it starts to thicken. Add lemon juice and beat until it forms soft peaks. Add vanilla. Gradually add sugar and beat until sugar dissolves and topping forms stiff peaks.

Emergency Baking

» Egg Substitutes

Common sense tells us we shouldn't attempt an omelet using these egg substitutes. However, they can be used in a pinch when making cookies or cakes. All of these egg substitutes are designed for use in baking only.

» ENER G Egg Replacer

This egg replacer is available in many supermarkets, often found in the health food section. Carefully read instructions for use. It has a shelf life of about three years and works quite well. Other egg substitutes may be available in your area.

Egg Substitute #1 (Flaxseed)

Yield: mix equals 1 egg

This inexpensive substitute works especially well in soft cookies such as sugar cookies, oatmeal cookies, and applesauce cookies, as well as muffins, quick breads, cakes, bar cookies, and so on, so store extra flaxseed in a cool, dry place. Don't replace more than two eggs in a recipe with flaxseed—too much flaxseed can make baked goods remain gummy inside. For each egg in the recipe, use this mix. No other adjustments are needed in the recipe.

1 Tbsp. ground flaxseeds   **3 Tbsp. water or other liquid**

Whisk or blend ingredients together and let mixture sit for about 5 minutes, until thick and gelatinous.

Tip: You can grind your own flaxseed in a heavy-duty blender or in a coffee grinder. Grind the seeds until they're fine, like a flaky powder. It is generally fine enough when the meal begins to clump together. A regular food processor may not achieve a fine enough grind.

Tip: Rancid flaxseed or flax meal tastes bitter and should not be used.

Egg Substitute #2

Yield: mix equals 1 egg

1 envelope Knox   **3 Tbsp. cold water**
**   unflavored gelatin**
                              2 Tbsp. boiling water

Before starting a recipe that requires eggs, sprinkle gelatin into cold water to soften for a few minutes. When soft, mix thoroughly with a spoon. Add boiling water and stir until dissolved. Refrigerate or place in freezer to thicken while preparing recipe. When the recipe calls for the addition of eggs, take the thickened gelatin and beat until frothy. This is of utmost importance. Then add to batter in place of one egg.

Egg Substitute #3

Yield: mix equals 1 egg

2 Tbsp. oil   **1 tsp. baking powder**
2 Tbsp. water

Combine oil, water, and baking powder. Whisk with fork until mixed. Use in place of one egg.

Egg Substitute #4

Yield: mix equals 1 egg

1 tsp. baking powder   **2 Tbsp. flour**
½ tsp. baking soda   **3 Tbsp. water**

Combine ingredients and mix together with a fork or whisk until foamy. Use in place of one egg.

Everlasting Yeast

A tip from Grandma: Don't ever use your last bit of yeast! Save it to make a new batch of Everlasting Yeast.

3–4 cups warm potato water or 2 Tbsp. dry potato flakes

1 quart water

1 Tbsp. instant dry yeast

2 Tbsp. sugar

1 tsp. salt

2 cups white or whole wheat flour

For potato water, scrub 1 potato, cut in pieces, and boil in 1 quart water until soft. Remove potato and cool water to lukewarm; add water if needed to equal 3–4 cups. Stir in yeast, sugar, salt, and flour. If using potato flakes, which also work well, stir them into the warm water with other ingredients. Put mixture in a 2-quart jar. Cover loosely with lid and set in warm place overnight to rise until ready to use for baking. Place jar in a bowl to catch overflow as mixture begins to rise. Stir occasionally to slow down the overflow. Use this mix, minus ½ cup, in chosen recipe. Be aware that this yeast mix will add flour to your recipe.

Tip: Save at least ½ cup of the everlasting yeast as a starter for the next batch of yeast. Between uses, keep yeast in a covered jar in the refrigerator until a few hours before needed.

When ready to use again: To the small amount of yeast starter saved from the last usage, add potato water or potato flakes and water, sugar, salt, and flour, following the basic recipe above. Do not add more yeast. Cover and set in warm place for a few hours or overnight before using. Do place jar in a bowl to catch the overflow as mixture begins to rise. And don't forget to stir the mixture occasionally.

Use desired amount in making bread or rolls. By keeping the everlasting yeast starter and remaking some each time, yeast can be kept on hand indefinitely. Be aware that dough rises more slowly using this yeast.

» Proofing

Proofing simply means testing your yeast (or baking powder or soda) to be sure it is active. If the expiration date on the package has passed, or if you're not sure that your yeast is active, always proof it before using. Vacuum-sealed packages of dry yeast that have been stored in a cool, dry place are often good for quite some time after the expiration date, even years in some cases. SAF-Instant yeast is highly recommended.

» To Proof Yeast

Dissolve 1 teaspoon dry yeast and 1 teaspoon sugar in warm water (110°F). Let the mixture stand for 6–12 minutes. If the mix begins to swell and foam, the yeast is alive. If yeast is active but a bit sluggish, simply use a little more dry yeast in the recipe. If you see no activity, discard the remainder of the package of dry yeast and begin with new yeast. There is absolutely no way to revive dead yeast, so don't use it!

» To Proof Baking Powder and Baking Soda

Baking powder: Stir 1 teaspoon baking powder into ⅓ cup hot water. If it fizzes a bit, it's still okay. If not, toss it out. Baking powder is often good long after the expiration date.

Baking soda: Stir ½ teaspoon baking soda into 1 tablespoon of vinegar or lemon juice. If it bubbles up like crazy, it's fine. If soda doesn't do much of anything, dispose of it (although it will still absorb odors in the refrigerator). Baking soda has a long shelf life.

CHAPTER 11

The Sick Bay

» Home Remedies and Therapeutic Recipes

"When you eat what nature offers, the reward is long life, happiness, health, wealth, and prosperity."

—Dr. George Blodgett

"Let food be thy medicine."

—Hippocrates

This chapter offers a variety of home remedies and therapeutic recipes that were gathered from many sources. They are for information only. They are not prescriptive in any way, but they offer helpful suggestions that have been used successfully through the years when medical help was unavailable.

Apple Cider Vinegar and Honey Cocktail

Excellent for digestion.

1 Tbsp. pure apple cider vinegar	8 oz. warm water
1 Tbsp. honey	¼–½ tsp. cayenne pepper, optional

Mix pure apple cider vinegar and honey in warm water and sip ½ hour before meals. Add cayenne to this drink if desired. Omit honey if diabetic.

Barley or Rice Water

Soothing and healing, particularly to the digestive system. Helps relieve diarrhea and helps rehydration. Barley is especially effective as a mild grain drink when prepared as Zip (p. XX).

1 cup barley or rice   **3 quarts pure water**

Place barley or rice and water in large stainless steel pan and simmer for about 2 hours. Cool, strain, and discard barley or rice. Drink the broth as needed.

Cough Suppressant

To stop nighttime coughing in a child or adult.

Vicks vapor rub

Put vapor rub generously on the bottom of the feet at bedtime (or nap time) and then cover with socks. It is also helpful to generously rub Vicks on the chest as well. Even persistent, deep, heavy coughing usually stops in about 5 minutes and can remain stopped for many hours of relief. Used in this way, Vicks vapor rub has an extremely soothing and calming effect on most people and aids sound sleep. This therapy is often a more effective treatment for children than even strong prescription cough medicines.

Disclaimer: This is not intended as a medical diagnosis. If condition persists or gets worse, seek medical help.

Flu-Survival Tea

A powerful herbal tea that seems to be especially effective in treating the prevalent viruses of today. Store herbs in a covered container in a cool, dry area until needed. This dry mix keeps well. You can find bulk herbs at www.sfherb.com.

chamomile	rose hips
comfrey leaf	yarrow
peppermint	red raspberry leaves
red clover	8 cups pure water

Use one tea bag or one tablespoon of each herb. Bring water to a boil in stainless steel saucepan. Add herbs, cover, and steep for 30–40 minutes. Let cool. Strain tea into large pitcher or jar. Cover and refrigerate. Drink one glass at a time, as often as desired. Drink at least 4 or more glasses a day for 3–4 days, or as needed. Tea is very effective. Double recipe if desired.

Mustard Plaster

A very effective remedy for chest congestion. It does not burn the skin when used as directed.

2 Tbsp. flour (doubled for an adult)	1 Tsp. dry mustard
	water

Combine ingredients to make a very thick paste. Prepare a piece of thin cotton cloth twice the size of the chest area. Spread paste on half the cloth, leaving the edges clear. Fold cloth in half, completely enclosing the mixture. Rub chest area liberally with petroleum jelly—if throat is sore, include base of throat. Lay plaster on chest but do not allow it to touch any skin that is not covered with petroleum jelly. Cover with plastic wrap if desired and then cover chest with a small towel. Keep patient warm and quiet for 20–30 minutes. The chest area will get warm and pink, but the mustard plaster should never burn the skin. After removing the plaster, keep patient warm and covered to prevent chilling. Repeat every 4 hours or as needed.

Oral Rehydration Solution

A simple and effective help for treating dehydration.

4 cups purified water   **½ tsp. salt**

2 Tbsp. sugar

Mix ingredients. Give person small sips of the solution every 5 minutes, even if they vomit, until they begin to urinate normally. The drink can be given with fruit juice as a flavoring.

Tip: Mix the dry ingredients for use during an emergency. The dry mix may be stored in a small container or plastic bag and added to 4 cups of water when needed. The mixture is handy to have in a 72-hour kit.

Parsley Tea

For kidney and bladder problems. Remarkable results have been reported.

4 cups water   **honey, optional**

**½ cup chopped fresh parsley or
   2–3 Tbsp. dried parsley**

Bring 4 cups water to a boil. Stir in parsley. Remove from heat, cover, and let steep for 10–15 minutes. Drink tea very warm but not scalding hot, and drink either strained or unstrained. Add honey if desired. Take up to 2 quarts of the parsley tea per day, or as needed.

Vegetable Broth

This cleansing, alkalinizing, and mineral-rich drink helps build and restore health.

2 large potatoes, chopped or sliced

2 carrots, chopped or sliced

2 celery stalks, including leaves, chopped

1 cup any other available vegetable (beet tops, parsley, or almost anything green and fresh), optional

8 cups water

Scrub vegetables but do not peel before chopping. Put all vegetables into a large stainless steel saucepan. Add water, cover, and bring to a boil. Then simmer for about 30 minutes. Cool until just warm, strain, and serve. If not used immediately, refrigerate, but warm before serving. Vegetables can be eaten or discarded.

» Wheatgrass

Dr. Ann Wigmore, a noted educator and founder of the Hippocrates Health Institute in Boston, has proven the extraordinary value of this vitamin and mineral-rich food in rebuilding health. More than one hundred elements from fresh wheatgrass have been isolated, and the researchers concluded that it is a complete food. Every known vitamin has been segregated from wheatgrass in the amounts and qualities best suited for use in the bodies of human beings. It is a body cleanser, rebuilder, and neutralizer of toxins. Wheatgrass is not a cure; it simply furnishes vital nourishment that the body needs to regenerate. Vegetables and fruits contaminated by sprays were cleansed and dangerous chemicals neutralized by the placing of wheatgrass in their wash water. Wigmore noted that wheatgrass gives protection against radiation and fall-out poisons when used in the bath and drinking water (Wigmore, *Be Your Own Doctor*).

Growing Wheatgrass

1 cup wheat   **2 cups peat moss**

pure water   **2–3 cups topsoil**

Put wheat in a quart jar. Fill with pure water and let soak at room temperature for 18–24 hours. Wheat can be planted immediately after soaking, but for best results, put soaked wheat into a sprouter or widemouthed quart jar. Turn the jar on its side and roll around to spread the wheat. Cover sprouter or jar with a cloth and let sprout for 24–36 hours. Rinse wheat with water and drain well at least twice a day to prevent spoilage.

Spread peat moss evenly in bottom of plastic greenhouse tray (or 9×3 baking dish) and dampen with water. Add topsoil and sprinkle with water until damp. Soil will be about 1 inch deep. Using a spatula, spread the sprouted wheat, leaving it thick and even on the soil (like icing a cake). Soak 8 layers of newspaper in water; lay this over the wheat. Wrap tray loosely with black plastic and put in a dark place. In 2–3 days, depending on room temperature, the sprouts will begin to raise the newspaper—they will be ½–¾ inches high and very white. Remove covering and place tray in full light. Water daily. Do not allow wheatgrass to dry out. Wheatgrass will begin to turn green almost immediately and will be 7–8 inches high and ready to cut in 8–10 days.

Harvesting Wheatgrass

Use a good pair of kitchen shears to cut wheatgrass close to the soil. Best if wheatgrass is used immediately, but it will keep in a plastic bag in the refrigerator for up to 1 week. To assure a continuous supply, start soaking more wheat when the previous tray of wheatgrass is about 2 inches high.

How to Use Wheatgrass

1. Cut wheatgrass into 1-inch lengths with scissors and add to green power smoothies. Eat as much as possible in salads and other uncooked dishes.

2. Cut wheatgrass into 1-inch lengths and juice in a good juicer, alternating wheatgrass and carrots.

Tip: Special electric and hand wheatgrass juicers are available.

Tip: Wheatgrass juice is concentrated, so it's best to dilute with water. Drink wheatgrass juice immediately after juicing for maximum benefit.

Wheat Milk

A nutritious drink that's very easy to make. Or use it over cereal. If you let wheat milk sit at room temperature for 24 hours, it tastes like buttermilk and is excellent for digestion.

1 cup 2-day wheat sprouts	**pinch of salt**
2 cups water or Zip **(next page)**	**honey**
	fresh fruit, optional

Blend wheat and water in blender for a few minutes. Strain and discard wheat. Add salt and sweeten with honey. Add fresh fruit if desired and blend again.

» Zip—A Mild Grain Drink

Zip is an energizing, enzyme-rich drink made from barley or wheat. Many prefer barley over wheat for this drink. Sometimes called a new form of acidophilus, it is an excellent digestive aid. Zip fortifies the immune system, and people who drink it regularly say it helps them avoid colds, flu, and viruses. Zip is beneficial for children as well as adults. If desired, mix this water with juice or use in smoothies

Zip

½ cup whole grain barley,
hull-less, or ½ cup whole
wheat kernels

1 quart pure water

Put barley or wheat in a widemouthed quart jar and fill with water. Do not cover. Let stand at room temperature for 24 hours. Drink the water. Add more water to the same grain and let stand another 24 hours. Again, drink the water. Repeat, using the same grain for 2–3 days and then discard and start with fresh grain.

» References

Back to Eden by Jethro Kloss

Be Your Own Doctor: A Positive Guide to Natural Living by Ann Wigmore

Bio-Kinetic Testing For Health: How to Take the Guesswork out of Healing by Tisha Mecham

Curing the Incurable: Vitamin C, Infectious Diseases, and Toxins by Thomas E. Levy, MD, JD

Eat to Live: The Amazing Nutrient-Rich Program for Fast and Sustained Weight Loss by Joel Fuhrman, MD

Feelings Buried Alive Never Die . . . by Karol K. Truman

Healthwise Handbook: A Self-Care Guide for You

Herbally Yours by Penny C. Royal

Home Nursing by the American Red Cross

Prescription for Nutritional Healing by Phyllis A. Balch, CNC

Set For Life: Eat More, Weigh Less, Feel Terrific! by Jane P. Merrill and Karen M. Sunderland

The China Study: Startling Implications for Diet, Weight Loss and Long-term Health by T. Colin Campbell, PhD

The Culprit & the Cure: Why Lifestyle Is the Culprit Behind America's Poor Health and How Transforming That Lifestyle Can Be the Cure by Steven G. Aldana, PhD

Wheat-free alternatives by Chef Brad at www.chefbrad.com

CHAPTER 12

Prepare for the Unexpected

I n an actual emergency "there's NO TIME to gather food from the kitchen, fill bottles with water, grab a first-aid kit from the closet and snatch a flashlight and portable radio from the bedroom. These items need to be packed and ready in one place before disaster strikes, because you might not have access to food, water and electricity for days or weeks" (Utah State University, *Emergency: Are You Prepared?*).

Store emergency supplies in one location that would be relatively safe from earthquakes and other disasters yet easily accessible if evacuation is required. Items can be stored in a five-gallon bucket with tight-fitting lid, suitcase and/or individual backpacks, and so on. Update clothes and food, and check batteries at least twice a year.

» In an Emergency

The information in this section comes from the American Red Cross, *Food and Water in an Emergency*.

» Water Is Essential

For water, one gallon per person per day is the minimum recommendation. That equals eight (sixteen-ounce) water bottles per person per day—four for drinking and four for cooking and other uses. If using dehydrated or freeze-dried foods, store plenty of additional water for their preparation.

» Types of Food Needed for an Emergency

The most useful foods in an energy emergency are those that require minimal preparation and cooking and no refrigeration. First, use up any perishable foods you have on hand, particularly in the refrigerator or freezer. Next, assess the types of food in your cupboard. Canned or bottled foods generally need little preparation other than mixing with water and heating. Most can be eaten cold if no heat is available. Food cans should be clean with no bulges. Bottles should be unbroken and clean.

» Low Food Supplies

"If activity is reduced, healthy people can survive on half their usual food intake for an extended period and without any food for many days. Food, unlike water, may be rationed safely, except for children and pregnant and nursing women.

"If your water supply is limited, don't eat salty foods, since they will make you thirsty. Instead, eat salt-free crackers, whole grain cereals, and canned foods with high liquid content." (American Red Cross, *Food and Water in an Emergency*, 6)

» Special Considerations

"As you stock food, take into account your family's unique needs and tastes. Familiar foods are important. They lift morale and give a feeling of security in times of stress. Try to include foods that they will enjoy and that are also high in calories and nutrition. Foods that require no refrigeration, water, special preparation, or cooking are best.

"Individuals with special diets and allergies will need particular attention, as will babies, toddlers, and the elderly. Nursing mothers may need liquid formula, in case they are unable to nurse. Canned dietetic foods, juices, and soups may be helpful for ill or elderly people.

"Make sure you have a manual can opener and disposable utensils. Don't forget non-perishable foods for your pets." (American Red Cross, *Food and Water in an Emergency*, 2–3)

Store extra water for your pets' needs. Have small plastic bags to clean up after them.

» Emergency Indoor Cooking

For safe indoor cooking, you can use a butane burner or standard fireplace in a well-ventilated room. Butane burners are compact, efficient, and inexpensive. They are popular for both general use and emergency backup—a must-have item for your emergency kit that you may not have. These stoves are also ideal to take camping.

Use a charcoal grill or camp stove outdoors only. Indoors, the fumes are lethal!

You can eat canned food directly out of the can.

» Food Supplies

Prepare a supply that will last two weeks. The easiest way to develop a two-week stockpile is to increase the amount of basic foods you normally keep on your shelves.

» Nutrition Tips

"During and immediately following a disaster, it will be vital that you maintain your strength. Remember the following:

- Eat at least one well-balanced meal each day.

- Drink enough liquid to enable your body to function properly (two quarts or a half gallon per day).

- Take in enough calories to enable you to do any necessary work.

- Include vitamin, mineral, and protein supplements in your stockpile to assure adequate nutrition." (American Red Cross, *Food and Water in an Emergency*, 6)

» Power-Outage Kit

1. A flashlight and extra batteries (hand-crank or solar flashlight). Have a least one good flashlight and an oil or battery-powered lamp or lantern.

2. Candles and matches. Candles are safe when set on a flat, stable, non-flammable surface.

3. A manual can opener and non-perishable food. Canned or instant soups, stews, and chili are good to have on hand. Protein or breakfast bars, crackers and peanut butter, and canned or dried fruit require no preparation and are good to have on hand also.

4. A cooler for storing frequently used foods. Food will keep several hours in a closed refrigerator and up to two days in the freezer, provided the door is not opened. Close that door in a hurry!

5. A supply of clean drinking water. You can fill sturdy plastic jugs with water and store them in empty spots in your freezer. They help keep food cold in the event of an outage and can be thawed if you run out of drinking water.

6. **A battery-powered radio and extra batteries,** or a solar or wind-up radio. If the outage is lengthy or associated with another emergency situation, radio reports will be issued regularly.

7. **Emergency phone numbers.** Keep numbers for your utilities, fire department, police department, and doctor handy. Before calling to report an outage, make sure your house hasn't just blown a fuse or tripped a circuit breaker. See if your neighbor's lights are off.

8. **A telephone that operates without electricity.** You must use a phone connected directly to the phone jack. Telephones with answering machines, as well as cordless phones, rely on electricity to operate.

9. **A first-aid kit and prescription medications.** If you take medication of any kind, make sure you have an ample supply.

10. **When the power goes out:**

    1. Reset your circuit breakers.

    2. Promptly turn off major appliances: air conditioner, dishwasher, television, computer, water heater, and so on.

» Grab-and-Go 72-Hour Emergency Kit

Recommendations in this section come from *Emergency: Are You Prepared?* with permission by Utah State University's extension service.

Store your kit close to an exit. Kit should include:

- Instruction manual on emergency preparedness

- Battery-powered, solar-powered or wind-up radio. Include batteries.

- Flashlight—battery-powered, solar-powered, or hand-crank—plus extra batteries if required

- First-aid kit and manual

- Sleeping bags and blankets (part wool, acrylic, or fleece)

- Personal hygiene needs

- Waterproof/windproof matches

- Essential medications

- Extra eye glasses/contacts and supplies

- Cell phone plus hand-crank charger

- Utility knife, pliers, wrench

- Infant and small children supplies, including diapers, wet wipes, etc., if applicable

- Supplies for elderly people, if applicable

- Manual can opener

- Non-perishable foods

- Water storage (vital)—1 gallon per person per day minimum, more if you have infants

- Change of clothing for each person, extra socks, jacket with hood. Store in plastic bags.

- Rain poncho or large garbage bag with hole cut for head to go through.

» Emergency Food Needs

Replace food in emergency kit every six to twelve months. Have enough non-perishable food for each family member to last at least seventy-two hours. Select foods that require no refrigeration, preparation, or cooking and little or no water. Consider storing snack pack–size fruits in juice, which provide extra liquid.

- Ready-to-eat foods in unbreakable containers

- Canned meats

- Juice, fruits, and vegetables

- Infant care foods

- Crackers, peanut butter

- High-energy foods such as granola and energy bars

- Comfort/stress foods—cookies, hard or soft candies, sweetened cereals, hot chocolate in individual packages, pudding in individual cups

- Paper cups, plates, napkins, paper towels, wipes, plastic utensils

» Other Emergency Needs

- Paper, pen, pencils, notebooks

- Leather work gloves

- Tools as desired

- Money. Include small bills, nothing larger than a five-dollar bill, and change such as quarters.

- Address and phone numbers of family and close friends

- Picture of you with your family for identification

- Laminated identification card stating name of person, address, parents, and contact information in case children or elderly people are separated from family members.

- List all family members living in the home so emergency responders will know who to look for.

» Stress Relievers

Children: Pencil, paper, puzzles, crayons, coloring books, games, soft stuffed animal, and soft blankets

Adults: Pencil, paper, notebook, book, magazines, games, needle-work, and soft blankets

» Important Records and Documents

Make copies of all legal papers and put in a waterproof, portable container.

- Family records and birth, marriage, and death certificates

- Health insurance—companies and contact information

- Medical information—name of doctors, phone numbers, any medications you are currently taking, health history, etc.

- House mortgage, vacation home/property ownership

- Automotive, motor home, trailers, snowmobiles, boat ownership

- Wills

- Insurance policies, contracts, deeds, stocks and bonds

- Passports, social security cards, immunization records

- Bank account numbers

- Credit card account numbers and companies

- Inventory of valuable household goods, pictures if possible

- Addresses and telephone numbers of relatives and other contacts

- Contact information for an out-of-state person who has all your information

» Additional Supplies

- Personal hygiene items including a toothbrush, toothpaste, lip balm, comb, brush, soap, towel, contact lens supplies, and feminine supplies. These items fit well in a ziplock bag.

- Toilet paper—flatten roll and put in ziplock bag

- A whistle to signal for help

- Needles, thread, small scissors

- Shut-off wrench for household gas and water

- Shovel and other useful tools

- ABC fire extinguisher

- Map of area

- Supplies for persons with special needs such as infants, elderly, or disabled persons

» Sanitation Kit

- Plastic bucket with tight-fitting lid
- Plastic bags and ties
- Disinfectant (bleach or Lysol)
- Improvised toilet seat
- Folding shovel
- Personal toiletries
- Toilet paper
- Hand sanitizer
- Paper towels
- Personal wipes
- Feminine hygienic needs
- Liquid soap
- Water

» Standard First-Aid Kit

- First-aid manual
- Aspirin or pain relievers, liquid and capsules
- Allergy medication—liquid and capsules
- Saline solution
- Laxatives
- Rubbing alcohol, alcohol wipes
- Diarrhea medicine
- Petroleum jelly
- Soap
- Hand sanitizer
- Salt and baking soda (½ tsp. soda, 1 tsp. salt in 1 quart water for shock)
- Gauze
- Adhesive bandages
- Antibiotic ointment
- Burn cream
- Triangular bandage (36×36×52)
- Elastic bandage
- Cotton balls

- Cotton swabs
- Safety pins
- Scissors
- Thermometer
- Sanitary napkins (pressure dressing)
- Disposable diapers (dressing/splint/padding)
- Adhesive, paper tape
- Matches
- Needles
- Tweezers
- Small splints, popsicle sticks
- Heavy string
- Syrup of ipecac
- Individual medical needs

» Car Mini-Survival Kit

- Always maintain at least ½ tank of gas in vehicle
- First-aid kit and manual
- Fire extinguisher, ABC type
- Bottled water
- Non-perishable, ready-to-eat foods in metal cans
- Flares and reflectors
- Blanket or sleeping bag
- Sealable plastic bags
- Battery-powered or hand-crank radio and flashlight
- Waterproof matches and candle in a jar or metal can with lid
- Essential medications

- Tools, screwdriver, pliers

- Jumper cables

- Short rubber hose for siphoning gas

- Small package of tissues

- Pre-moistened towelettes

- Local maps

- Extra clothes

- Sturdy shoes and good socks

Create a Family Disaster Plan

(From *Emergency: Are You Prepared?* with permission.)

- Have a family meeting place outside the home in case of disaster.

- Fire drill—determine escape routes and practice at least yearly.

- Conduct calm family discussions about earthquakes and other possible disasters.

- Demonstrate and talk about what to do in each situation.

- Practice the plan so everyone will remember what to do when a disaster happens.

- Know the school emergency plan; make sure your child knows the plan.

- Know your workplace emergency plan, make sure your spouse knows as well

- Help children memorize family name, address and phone number

- Teach children what to take with them in an emergency, including a bag by their bed and their 72-hour kit near exit

- Make sure children know what smoke detectors, fire alarms and local community warning systems sound like

» Children's Response to an Emergency

(From *Emergency: Are You Prepared?* with permission.)

Roles

- **Adult reaction:** In a disaster, children will look to you and other adults for help. How you react to an emergency gives them clues on how to act.

- **Stay in control.** Adults must stay in control of the situation, and remember that their response during this time may have a lasting impact.

- **Children depend on daily routines.** They wake up, eat breakfast, go to school, and play with their friends. When emergencies or disasters interrupt this routine, they may become anxious.

- **Maintain discipline.** Be firm and supportive.

- **Children's Feelings:** Adults should take a child's fears seriously. Provide reassurance by talking with them and presenting an honest, realistic picture.

- **Children's Fears:** Recognize their concerns, such as the event may happen again, someone may be injured or killed, they may be separated from the family, they may be left alone.

After the Emergency

- Concentrate on the child's emotional needs by talking with them about their feelings. Try to reduce your child's fear and anxiety.

- Keep the family together. Calmly and firmly explain all situations as best you can. Tell children what you know about the disaster. Explain what will happen next; for example, "Tonight, we will all stay together in the shelter."

- Let children talk about the disaster and ask questions as much as they want. Encourage children to describe what they're feeling. Listen to what they say. If possible, include the entire family in the discussion.

- Include children in recovery activities. Give children chores that are their responsibility. This helps them feel they are part of the recovery. Having a task helps them understand that eventually things will be all right.

- If a child does not respond to the above suggestions, seek help from a mental health specialist or member of the clergy.

- -

Play Dough

Children respond to calming activities such as playing with play dough. This is a simple recipe that makes up in minutes.

2 cups water

3 Tbsp. oil

1 Tbsp. alum or cream of tartar

8–10 drops food coloring, if desired

2½ cups white flour

½ cup salt

Bring water, oil, alum or cream of tartar, and food coloring to a boil. Remove from heat. Mix flour and salt. Stir into hot water and knead until smooth. Dough should be very soft and workable. Keeps well.

Tip: Dough keeps best with mineral oil or baby oil, but cooking oil can be used.

» Fuel Storage and Consumption Rates

Fuels will be important in an emergency. Gas lines, electricity, and refineries are often interrupted in cases of earthquakes and other disasters. Emergency fuel supplies and safe ways to use them are necessary.

Avoid storing gas, kerosene, or similar fuels where they might be dangerous to the house or people. Keep them out of children's reach. Never store fuel near food or water; an offensive taste will generally result. Wood or coal are safe to store and are useful in fireplaces and emergency stoves.

Listed below are certain pieces of equipment and their approximate fuel-consumption rates.

Portable Butane Burner and Lantern (Use Indoors or Outdoors)

Burner: 1 butane fuel cartridge burns for 4 hours on medium, 5–6 hours on low.

Lantern: 1 butane fuel cartridge burns for 10–12 hours.

Candles

¾-inch diameter × 4-inch height: 2 hours 20 minutes

⅞-inch diameter × 4-inch height: 5 hours

2 inches square × 9 inches tall: 7 hours per inch or 63 hours, which figures to be nearly 2 weeks at 5 hours per day

Flashlight (Two Batteries)

Continuous running on new batteries: 5–7 hours

Old batteries: 3–4 hours

Gas Lantern (Coleman Two-Mantle)

Burning at the rate of 5 hours per day, the following amount of white gas would be used:

- 1 pint per day

- 4 quarts per week

- 4 gallons per month

Kerosene Lantern (1-Inch Wick)

A kerosene lantern will burn for about 45 hours on 1 quart. Burning at the rate of 5 hours a day, the following amounts of kerosene would be used:

- ½ cup per day

- 1 quart per week

- 1 gallon per month

- 12 gallons per year

Two-Plate Gas Burner (Camp Stove)
(Outdoor Use Only)

With both burners burning 4 hours per day, the following amounts of fuel would be used:

- 1 quart per day

- 2 gallons per week

- 8 gallons per month

Caution: Using or storing highly flammable or any other combustible material in or around the house is not recommended. Use all type of burning fuel only where well ventilated.

BIBLIOGRAPHY

Airola, Paavo. *How to Get Well: Dr. Airola's Handbook of Natural Healing.* N.p.: Health Pub Plus, 1984.

American Academy of Pediatrics. "Switching to Solid Foods." Healthychildren.org. Last modified May 28, 2013. http://www .healthychildren.org/English/ages-stages/baby/feeding-nutrition /Pages/Switching-To-Solid-Foods.aspx.

American Red Cross. *Food and Water in an Emergency.* Last modified May 2006. http://www.redcross.org/images/MEDIA _CustomProductCatalog/m4440181_Food_and_Water-English .revised_7-09.pdf.

Franz, Kay B., and Cresson H. Kearny. *Maintaining Nutritional Adequacy During a Prolonged Food Crisis.* Oak Ridge, TN: Oak Ridge National Laboratory, 1979. http://web.ornl.gov/info /reports/1979/3445600218930.pdf.

National Association of Wheat Growers. "Fast Facts." Accessed September 4, 2013. http://www.wheatworld.org/wheat-info/fast -facts/.

Utah State University Cooperative Extension. *Emergency: Are You Prepared?* Accessed September 4, 2013. http://extension.usu.edu /weber/files/uploads/Emergency%20Are%20You%20Prepared2 .pdf.

————. *"Use It or Lose It!": Food Storage Cooking School,* 2nd Ed. Logan, UT: Utah State University, 1999. http://extension.usu .edu/files/publications/publication/FN_503.pdf.

Wigmore, Ann. *Be Your Own Doctor: A Positive Guide to Natural Living,* 2nd Ed. N.p.: Avery, 1982.

INDEX

About the Authors

Jane P. Merrill is an author, presenter, and professional health and weight control counselor. She has taught both as an independent consultant and as owner and operator of three health and weight control centers and a Bosch kitchen store. Jane has taught many cooking, nutrition, food storage, and preparedness classes based upon simple, practical methods of food preparation using basic foods. She believes in eating well without spending all day in the kitchen. For many years she has encouraged personal and family preparedness. Jane is the wife of Jay W. Merrill and mother of six children. They have twenty-eight grandchildren and thirty-eight great-grandchildren, and still counting!

Karen M. Sunderland is an author and presenter and has a bachelor's degree in family and consumer science, with an emphasis in nutrition. She has taught many cooking, food storage, and preparedness classes, encouraging all to be prepared for the unexpected. Karen has coauthored 3 cookbooks with her mother Jane, and is the author of one cookbook on her own. Karen is the wife of Merrill Sunderland and mother of six children. They have sixteen grandchildren with more to come.

Authors' Contact Information
Email: feastingonfoodstorage@gmail.com
Website: www.feastingonfoodstorage.com